FIRST THINGS FAST

"Rossett's book is a practical, down-to-earth set of guidelines from an accomplished professional who has obviously 'been there.'"

> — **Joe Harless, author, *Peak Performance System* and *The Eden Conspiracy: Educating for Accomplished Citizenship***

"Rossett has produced an eminently readable, practical handbook that helps human resource professionals apply performance analysis methods fast. A friendly, comforting, useful volume that we will definitely recommend to our clients."

> — **Harold D. Stolovitch, professor, Université de Montréal; president, Harold D. Stolovitch & Associates; and Erica J. Keeps, executive vice-president, Harold D. Stolovitch & Associates**

"Rossett's new book is a wonderful blend of basic principles and illustrative examples from educational, governmental, and corporate settings. It will be on the bookshelf of all professionals concerned with improving performance in organizations. *First Things Fast* is tightly written with no wasted words. Each chapter provides you with fundamental guidelines you need to conduct a timely performance analysis. I plan to include this book in all my needs assessment seminars."

> — **Ruth Clark, principal, Clark Training & Consulting; former president, International Society for Performance Improvement**

"A timely, pragmatic tool. The speed of change in the business environments in which performance analysis is practiced demands frequent definition of problems and opportunities. *First Things Fast* builds on Rossett's previous sound work while meeting the urgent challenge of speed."

> — **Sandy Quesada, director of global training and development, Eli Lilly and Company**

"This book is a must-have for anyone who is responsible for identifying performance and training needs. It's chock full of proven tips, techniques, practices, tools, and examples. And with Rossett's wonderful humor evident throughout, it's fun to read!"

> — **Dana Gaines Robinson, president, Partners in Change; coauthor, *Performance Consulting: Moving Beyond Training***

FIRST THINGS FAST

A Handbook for
Performance Analysis

Allison Rossett

Foreword by Marc J. Rosenberg

San Francisco

Copyright © 1999 by Jossey-Bass/Pfeiffer

ISBN: 0–7879–4438-6

Library of Congress Cataloging-in-Publication Data

Rossett, Allison.
    First things fast : a handbook for performance analysis /
Allison Rossett.
    p.   cm.
    Includes index.
    ISBN 0-7879-4438-6
    1. Performance standards.   2. Task analysis.   3. Employees—Training of.
4. Training needs.   I. Title.
    HF5549.5.P35 R67 1998
    658.4'013—ddc21   98-25301

Printed in the United States of America
Published by

350 Sansome Street, 5th Floor
San Francisco, California 94101-1342
(415) 433-1740; Fax (415) 433-0499
(800) 274-4434; Fax (800) 569-0443

Visit our Web site at www.pfeiffer.com

Acquiring Editor: Larry Alexander
Director of Development: Kathleen Dolan Davies
Copyeditor: Michele Jones
Senior Production Editor: Dawn Kilgore
Manufacturing Supervisor: Becky Carreño
Cover Design: Brenda Duke

Printing 10 9 8 7 6 5 4 3 2 1

CONTENTS

◆ FOREWORD

"If you don't know where you're going, any place will do."

FROM Alice in Wonderland

We've all been there. Trying to solve problems we haven't defined. Grabbing at solutions because they seem right or they worked once before. Delivering a product to the field in spite of that nagging sense that you just aren't quite sure why the product was developed in the first place. And then, of course, suffering the consequences when things don't work the way we'd hoped.

It's no wonder training has traditionally gotten a bad rap. We focus on outputs not solutions, they tell us. We embrace glitzy multimedia, sometimes at the expense of learning. We're more concerned with student days than student performance.

In many ways, training became like the U.S. automobile industry of the 1970s and 1980s—pushing lots of product out the back door that ignored the needs of consumers and generally didn't work well or last very long. But the auto industry recently came roaring back by spending more time understanding the requirements of customers and building products that didn't just look good but worked extremely well and provided lasting satisfaction.

In our business, we've also changed. We're putting more emphasis on performance analysis. Why? Because like the car manufacturers of twenty years ago, we want not only to survive, but to grow and prosper. We need to better understand the underlying problems and requirements of those who will use our products. What are their concerns and their reality? What results are they looking for? What do we need to know to assure that what we do will work?

Performance analysis tools and methodologies have proliferated in recent years. Indeed, one of Allison Rossett's previous books, *Training Needs Assessment*, provides a strong foundation for this new direction. Performance analysis, part of an emerging human performance technology, has also given us a wider field of vision, to see beyond training solutions to a host of other interventions that provide valid and cost-effective ways to improve workplace performance. Performance analysis has been embraced by professional training and human resource societies. It's being taught at most universities. But most important, it's being recognized as an important business tool.

There's just one problem. It takes too long. Or, it's perceived to take too long. In an era of ever-decreasing cycle times and shorter product life cycles, the ability to make quick decisions regarding performance improvement, including training, becomes paramount. Although performance analysis helps us overcome the Alice in Wonderland effect of not knowing where we are going, it's still regarded as too slow, and, quite frankly, often a pain. There's a great deal of evidence that this is the primary reason why performance analysis is not done.

In *First Things Fast: A Handbook for Performance Analysis*, Allison Rossett tackles cycle time head-on. Although Rossett maintains her healthy reliance on data-based decision making, she presents some interesting ways to get there. For me, the book provides a number of keen insights:

First, act like a detective rather than a scientist. Find the big nuggets of information. Deduce possible outcomes. Look for clues and trends in behavior. Accumulate evidence rather than proof, estimates rather than exactness. This will speed things up without significant loss of data integrity.

Second, rely on others. Rossett makes a big case for partnering. Not only does this enable the client to feel part of the effort, and thus take more ownership of the results, but it recognizes a key element of increasing the efficiency of the work: the client knows a lot of stuff. Find information that already exists. Talk to people who are in a position to know what's going on. If you pick the right people and you get consistent responses, you're likely on the right track.

Third, use tools and technology. Improving the *productivity* of performance analysis is the essence of this book. Don't re-invent the wheel each time you go out. If the tools and technology you have at your disposal aren't perfect, refine them over time. The point here is to build a process and a capability that can be replicated in many situations. This saves time.

Finally, refine as you go. Things change, and they change often. A performance analysis "set in stone," with all the details anyone could possibly want, may be of little value a week from now when the business situation is turned on its head by a new competitor or the budget for the solution you had planned is cut in half. Perfection is costly and may not be all it is cracked up to be. Better to analyze just enough to be comfortable making the next set of decisions and keep revisiting your assumptions and findings throughout the project.

As George Stalk and Thomas Hout note in their 1990 book, *Competing Against Time*, businesses are driven by three major criteria: cost, quality, and responsiveness, or speed. In the automotive industry in recent years, Chrysler's mantra has been substantially shortened development cycle times and time to market, both responsiveness measures. The result is a resurgent, highly competitive company and a leader in a more competitive industry. Likewise, the performance improvement industry must also look at responsiveness as a critical success factor.

Performance analysis has always sought to help organizations drive down cost and increase quality by assuring that the solutions recommended are, in fact, what is truly needed. The beauty of this book is that it recognizes the critical nature of speed in doing performance analysis work, without sacrificing the other measures. Performance analysis is at the center of a training industry driving toward a fundamental transformation. *First Things Fast: A Handbook for Performance Analysis* is your road map.

September 1998

Marc J. Rosenberg
Senior Consultant
OmniTech Consulting Group

◆ PREFACE

I wrote this book because the topic of analysis, which can be thought of as the planning essential to human resources and training, remains an itch that just won't go away. Carl Czech and I (Rossett & Czech, 1996) once conducted a small study that demonstrated that although professionals value analysis, many admit to not doing much or even any of it. And Cathy Tobias and I just completed a related study, not yet published, with only slightly more optimistic results.

While books, articles, and speeches abound, it's not a stretch to describe analysis as attracting more heat than light. Why is that?

- *Leaders often prefer a quick fix.* Most executives want what they want when they want it, not after a study of the matter.
- *Analysis is even less interesting to leaders in organizations than training is.* Few executives want to talk about training and fewer still are intrigued with the planning associated with realizing opportunities or solving problems. Their eyes glaze over.
- *There is little history in the organization of analyses that have made noticeable dents in what matters.* Even the telling results of fine analysis studies are often lost in the excitement of rolling out reengineered processes, a new recognition program, and just the right training. Too often, the data gathering and involvement of sources are lost. And that's

when such excellent studies even exist. It's not hard to find professionals who can't point to a single result of their planning efforts aside from the frustration of the impatient customer.

- *Your customers think they know what they need.* Accustomed to leading, many customers refrain from posing a problem or challenge and instead leap to habitual solutions, often those that are single interventions, like training or documentation.

- *The measurements don't match.* Few human resources and training professionals are measured by the *eventual* impact they make on strategic goals or even the *subsequent* delight of the customers they serve. When measurements are taken, most are still fixed on those variables that are easy to discern, like people in attendance or the number of meetings that are facilitated.

- *People don't know what analysis is.* There is little agreement about what constitutes effective planning, whether you call it analysis, scoping, diagnostics, auditing, needs analysis, needs assessment, or performance analysis. Nobody enjoys the confusion, least of all the customer we hope will provide resources for it.

- *Analysis isn't easy to do.* It involves many challenges, from figuring out how to plan, to convincing sources to participate, to collecting data, to figuring out what the data mean, to making the findings matter in the organization. Political and cognitive skills are tapped during analysis.

- *Analysis takes time and time is in short supply.* Little explanation is necessary here. We all know the number one reason for avoiding analysis—there's no time for it.

This book attempts to address each of these barriers. It is meant to be a practical guide to handling every one of them through examples, explanations, tools, and templates. If you're new to the field, this handbook will help you anticipate resistance and deal with it. If you're a veteran, I hope you'll appreciate my efforts to bring clarity and concreteness to an often murky topic. I do this by telling stories and offering dialogues about our business. Some are true. Some are imaginary. All will sound familiar or possible.

I've always enjoyed Greek mythology, thanks to Edith Hamilton (1993). I've taken that appreciation into my current work, continuing to savor themes that put people at the heart of the story, that recognize flashes of the monstrous and miraculous in most circumstances and individuals, and that honor the critical struggle to make the unknown known.

Isn't this what performance analysis is about?

I hope that this book helps you ask and answer better questions for yourself and for your organization.

September 1998   Allison Rossett
                                                                                        San Diego, California

◆ ACKNOWLEDGMENTS

I've learned important lessons from my academic colleagues and students at San Diego State University. I could not have smarter colleagues. In particular, I want to thank Pat Harrison, Margie Kitano, and Pam Monroe for many kinds of inspiration and support.

One blessing of teaching at the university has been my contact with generations of graduate students in educational technology at SDSU. Some have read chapters from this book and offered suggestions. Others provided the grist for the tales that pepper the book. I appreciate the work that Rebecca Vaughan and Mark Fulop did to improve the book.

I've continued to work with many of our alumni long after their graduation. Their ideas and support continue to be critical to my work: Terry Bickham, Carl Czech, Joan Wackerman, Jim Marshall, Jeanne Strayer, Cathy Keenan, Kathy McCreary, Susan Madeiros, Marty Murillo, Ann Derryberry, Jeremy Barnett, Josh Siegel, Fernanda Gimenez-Groenendijk, Randy Bland, Kendra Sheldon, Lynn Richards, Marcie Bober, Judy Blum, Jeff Brechlin, Nancy Dosick, Jan Garbosky, Jeannette Gautier-Downes, Steve Eckols, Craig Ellsworth, Shirley Gresham, Chris Hall, Gene Adgate, Liz Herrick, Pam Morais, and Lou Sanchez.

Many colleagues deserve acknowledgment. Some posed interesting consulting problems on which we worked together, others helped me through their writings and other professional contributions, still others have been wonderful conversationalists: Paul Harmon, Roger Addison, Peter Dean, Diana Davis, Walt Dick, Bob Reiser, Marcie Driscoll, Jillian Dorman, Art Shirk, Judith Fidler, Joe Durzo, Marguerite Foxon, Ellen Wagner, Tom Stewart, Howard Lewis, Rob Foshay, John Stormes, Kathy Dardes, Marta de la Torre, Margaret MacLean, Darrell Gibson, Butch Henderson, Stefan Bauer, Sandy Quesada, Janice Simmons, Dave Merrill, Roger Kaufman, David Holcombe, Heidi Fisk, Gloria Gery, Joe and Julie Hymes, Ruth Stiehl, Dick Swanson, Jim Harwood, Ann Leon, Leanne Drennan, Amanda Scott, Katie Smith, Pat Kelly, Diane Musha, Brian Patterson, Pat Weger, Bill Brandon, Peggy Piz, Karen Kennedy, Dreama Perry, and Ken Finley.

I'd also like to acknowledge the antecedents of this book in what Robert Mager, Joe Harless, Tom Gilbert, Marc Rosenberg, Dave Merrill, Harold Stolovitch, Erica Keeps, Ruth Clark, and Ron Zemke have written and said. Their contributions are woven into the way I approach my work.

I've acknowledged many people. There are others. I apologize that you are not included in these long lists. You know who you are.

Finally, I want to thank Sue Reynolds for everything, absolutely everything.

◆ ◆ ◆

CHAPTER ONE

INTRODUCTION

You probably work in an organization that is very little like it was a few years ago. You are expected to adapt to these changes and, as a human resources professional, maybe even to provide leadership. The only certainty is more change in the future.

Just a few words provide a picture of the shifts you know so well: *performance, results, technology, measurements, accountability, billability, cross-functionality, technology,* and *consultation.* Where once human resources and training professionals enjoyed a niche defined and measured by familiar activities, such as offering classes or facilitating meetings, now there are expectations about contributing to results, the bottom line, the core business of the organization. In the past, each year a successful professional might publish an ever-larger course catalogue. Now, in more and more settings and possibly in far-distant countries with colleagues whose first language she does not share, this same professional is consulting with line units and tailoring efforts to help clients accomplish their goals.

What do these changes mean for you? They mean being driven by customers and causes, not by history, habit, or job title. They mean customizing services to needs and opportunities. They mean gathering data and perceptions from associates, managers, experts, leaders, and benchmarking groups. They mean scrutinizing data to divine solutions. They mean cobbling together solution systems. They mean working cross-functionally. The basis for all these activities is performance analysis. Performance analysis gives you the understanding you need to chart a fresh and tailored approach.

Is This Book for You?

This book is for you if you've found yourself thinking,

> I don't know where to start.
>
> What's performance analysis? Why should I bother?
>
> A certain amount of analysis is critical, I guess. What would be best? OK, what's the minimum?
>
> They've reorganized our unit, and now I'm in this unit called "client relationships," and we're supposed to be doing performance consulting. What should we do?
>
> How do I avoid analysis-paralysis?
>
> This is just a small part of my job. I don't have time for all of this assessment stuff.
>
> My customer says she knows what she needs and that it's not analysis. How can I make a case for study prior to action?
>
> They want some courses, and one customer wants Web-based training. But I have my doubts about whether an isolated course, in the classroom or through high technology, is going to solve this problem. How can I make them see this?

The challenges are numerous: skepticism from clients; time pressures; limited analysis know-how; unfamiliar roles in changing organizations; cultural, language, and time zone differences; and expectations regarding cost recovery and collaborations across units. Whereas the traditional roles of human resources and training were functional, tactical, and blissfully familiar, this new world of performance analysis, consultation services, and solution systems is more fluid and strategic. It demands more of you. The changes won't be easy, but they are absolutely essential—for the organization and for you.

That sentence ends the sympathy. From here on we'll talk about how to think about and succeed in these new roles and services, and we'll focus on analysis as the strategy to enable you to do just that.

This book is written for human resources and training professionals who are eager to choose solutions based on the situation, not their inclination; who are interested in analysis prior to action; who seek to consult with line organizations to establish field-based cases for their recommendations; and who are operating under time constraints. Many are called trainers by their organizations. Some are internal or external organizational developers and process reengineers. A few call themselves instructional designers or performance consultants or even performance technologists. Some have another position entirely but find themselves tasked with or attracted to solving problems. Still others are human resources generalists. What all share is a desire to shift from predetermined activities and events to consultation and customized solutions. They are working to establish business partnerships. Their efforts begin with performance analysis.

Performance Analysis and Needs Assessment?

In the past I've written about needs assessment in a way that defines it as a large, overarching concept that is arguably synonymous with good human resources planning. Although I still hold by that definition, I was, I fear, overly optimistic about the welcome that such a demanding process would receive in the field. As practical experience and numerous studies of practice have shown, needs assessment is honored more in theory than in practice. What to do? Do we abandon this critical planning simply because so many report that they fail to do much of it? I don't think so.

I'm no longer convinced it is helpful to define needs assessment so broadly, because when you do, a commitment to needs assessment will necessitate the expenditure of significant resources up front. Professionals run up against a wall of resistance when they attempt to gather so much information from so many sources at the get-go. Instead, I'm proposing that we reduce the daunting size of the effort by carving the planning process into more manageable and iterative bite sizes: one swift, targeted bite up front and then subsequent mouthfuls of assessment for subsequent associated programs.

It's hard to argue with the hundreds who've said in one way or another, "Sure, I'm for assessment. I just don't get to do it. What else do you have for me? I want to make better decisions, do some planning, but not jump into so much study." What I have for this typical professional is performance analysis, that smaller, focused bite.

Performance analysis, then, becomes the front end of the front end. It is an elegant gaze at the situation. It matches organizational changes that are now emerging in human resources and training organizations, such as those of SBC and IBM, in which a group of professionals, who might be called relationship consultants, requirements consultants, or performance consultants, are serving strategic roles. They work close to customers and continuously scan and respond, turning projects over to other human resources and training professionals, depending on the challenge or opportunity. Their job is to swiftly figure things out, as Ron Zemke of *Training* magazine put it in his classic text, *Figuring Things Out* (Zemke & Kramlinger, 1982). What these professionals are doing is performance analysis, a precursor to the substantial planning involved in the needs assessment associated with the production of a particular solution, like a class or a reenginered policy or a multimedia program.

Only after it is certain that a training, coaching, or information solution is appropriate does the organization make the investment in more substantial training needs assessment. Table 1.1 shows a brief comparison of performance analysis and training needs assessment.

In the table, note the difference in why, when, and how. In performance analysis, we are attempting to make a preliminary sketch of the opportunity, to figure out what is involved in serving a customer, and then to bring the necessary partners together to collaborate on the solution system. Performance analysis is what we do before we invest in needs assess-

TABLE 1.1. PERFORMANCE ANALYSIS
AND TRAINING NEEDS ASSESSMENT.

Performance Analysis	*Training Needs Assessment*
Is a process for partnering with clients to figure out what it will take to achieve their goals	Is a process for determining what is in and what is out of an instructional or informational program
Results in a data-driven rationale and the description of a solution system	Results in classes, job aids, coaching, documentation, electronic performance support, and so on
Is an initial response to the opportunity or request from the client or customer	Is a follow-on study that takes performance analysis findings and turns them into the "right" instruction and information
Focuses on defining the limits of the problem or domain in broad strokes and then determining what to do	Focuses on texture and authenticity, on what performers need to know and do *in detail*
Defines the opportunity or problem and what to do about it	Defines the details necessary to create concrete solutions
Defines cross-functional solution systems	Identifies the details of exemplary performance and perspectives so that they can be taught, included in knowledge-management systems, and communicated

ment or what we can finally, accurately dub training needs assessment. Once we have determined that education, training, or information will contribute, the lengthier training needs assessment can commence. Performance analysis guarantees doing the right things. Needs assessment or training needs assessment is about doing those right things right.

This book focuses on performance analysis. My previous book, *Training Needs Assessment,* covers the more extensive efforts and in more detail. See Chapter Two for more discussion of these two concepts.

There are precedents for chopping the front end into targeted and related parts, where what you learn in the first phase enlightens subsequent efforts. General practitioners, for example, do it when a patient presents with a problem like fatigue. They ask questions to determine likely causes and then turn to more extensive testing to confirm educated hunches. Subsequent contact with specialists, and related intensive diagnostics, are based on that initial once-over.

Another example is the early opportunity analysis conducted by entrepreneurs. In real estate development, an experienced developer quickly reviews the characteristics of a potential site to identify the issues most likely to be fatal to the project. Using as little time and money as possible, the developer confirms the "deal-killer" issue and moves on to another site, or finds that the issue is tolerable and moves on to the next potential deal killer for that site. Only when the largest, easiest-to-investigate killers are retired does the developer invest "real" money and time in the project.

Let's look at some questions and concerns you might have. Table 1.2 summarizes the concerns and responds to them.

How Does the Book Work?

In this chapter and in Chapters Two and Three, I define performance analysis and explain why, why now, why you, and why so quickly. I provide the performance analysis basics, along with examples, job aids, and templates.

Chapter Four focuses on handling typical situations, such as a request for support in the introduction of new software or the need to plan to ensure that engineers' skills remain contemporary. The chapter highlights four kinds of requirements: (1) a rollout of a new system, approach, or perspective; (2) a problem with performance or results; (3) development for a particular group of people; and (4) strategic planning. We will look at strategies for carrying out performance analysis that are linked to these quintessential requests for assistance.

Chapter Five highlights speed. It describes strategies for putting the pedal to the metal and reviews ways of capturing useful data without large numbers of sources or lengthy processes.

Chapter Six acknowledges that performance analysis is a planning process with two primary purposes. The first is to figure out what needs to be done to serve the client and organization. The second is to establish relationships in the organization and readiness for subsequent interventions. In this chapter, while reviewing interviews, focus groups, observation, and surveys as methods for performance analysis, we concentrate

TABLE 1.2. CONCERNS ABOUT SPEEDY PERFORMANCE ANALYSIS.

Concerns	Responses
"I like needs assessment. Will I still get to do it?"	Of course. Performance analysis sets the table for needs assessment, finding the right places to direct that focused study. In some organizations, the analyst passes the project on to others who will do the needs assessment. In others, the work is done by the same person.
"It would take me hours to figure out how to do this performance analysis."	This handbook will provide templates matched to the kinds of opportunities you're likely to have. Adapting the template and sample questions will shave time off your study. Use the book in a just-in-time way, if you prefer. Besides, you owe yourself the professional development.
"This doesn't give me enough time."	PA probably doesn't give you enough time to feel certain. What it will do is give you a general picture of what's happening, enabling you to recommend likely, but not certain, directions and approaches. Remember, PA is the beginning, not the end, of your work with your customers.
"I have projects in Palo Alto; Togo, Africa; and Singapore. Will this planning process help me?"	I intend it to. We'll talk about the issues that many countries, cultures, and settings impose on you. Although there are no easy answers, there are some strategies, including the use of technology, that will address issues raised by distance and difference.
"I prefer surveys. Can I do one in performance analysis?"	Yes, you can, especially if you are seeking priority directions, and after you've done sufficient study to be able to present options in the survey. Technology is also useful here. See Chapter Seven for ideas about how to use technology to speed up and extend your reach.
"Performance analysis. Needs assessment. Get serious. My management won't give me that much time."	Take the bull by the horns. Although it is difficult to justify lengthy studies, it is even more difficult to justify hasty actions. Use architects and doctors as analogies. Would your customer respect a physician or architect who plunged into surgery or a building project without diagnostics?

on the perspectives of executives, managers, employees, experts, and solution partners during analysis.

Chapter Seven looks at technology and analysis. This chapter describes how people are beginning to use technologies both to gather and to analyze data and offers suggestions to increase electronic participation. It discusses technology basics, such as e-mail interviews, and extends to more exotic possibilities, such as Web-based focus groups.

Chapter Eight describes ways to present the results of your performance analyses and includes examples of both a performance analysis report and a briefing for a group of executives. This chapter discusses the challenges related to influencing others and presents touchstones for turning analysis efforts into action in the organization.

In Chapter Nine, five people tell about their experiences with analysis. A variety of professionals describe what happened, why they think it happened, and what they'd do differently if they had it to do over again. Their experiences take us to foreign countries, into elementary school classrooms, and to the worlds of finance, fish, franchising, technology innovation, and consulting.

Chapter Ten describes trends in our business and how they relate to performance analysis. A glossary and a source and reference listing are at the end of the book.

This is a handbook, with the following characteristics:

- It's handy. The book is meant to be easy to use. It responds to the needs of two kinds of people: those who want to do performance analyses and those who don't yet want to but might, given good tools and reasons. The book is oriented to your challenges, questions, successes, and concerns.
- It's functional. If you want to know where to start on a performance analysis, the options are here. If you want a sample executive interview for a technology rollout, you can find one to tailor to your situation. If you are confronting resistance from experts, you'll find an example here that's similar to what you're experiencing and suggestions for how to respond.

- It's chock full of practical stuff. There are many examples, charts, anecdotes, and quotes. Job aids are everywhere. There are also exceptions and irreverent commentary.

- It includes the voice of the customer. Sprinkled throughout the book are typical conversations and anecdotes. There are dialogues between trainers, performance analysts, customers, and experts. They provide a quick way to witness and thus prepare for the perspectives of others and for what you have confronted or will confront when you plan.

- It's stripped down. I've vacuumed out nonessential details. I've eliminated introductions and foundational materials. Unfortunately, this means I've pulled out many references. I apologize to the wise people whose thinking has influenced this book (such as Joe Harless, Robert Mager, Peter Pipe, Tom Gilbert, Geary Rummler, Marc Rosenberg, Ruth Clark, Ron Zemke, and many others) for not making the frequent allusions to their contributions that I've offered in earlier writings. My purpose here is to make it easier for human resources professionals to get their jobs done—to get to the heart of the matter, as Robert Mager put it (1970). The references that are included are meant to provide more perspectives and examples, not historical underpinnings.

- It's relevant. We'll visit computer companies, banks, oceans, and government agencies. We'll talk about sales, diversity, teams, software, and management development in this country and others. We'll talk about the implications of global settings for analysis. Examples and dialogues come from real projects in real organizations, and, where possible, I will identify the company or agency. Often, I'll take experiences and combine and even exaggerate them to illustrate points. Given the choice of several examples or quotes, I'll pick the more irreverent.

- It's fun. Well, maybe *fun* is too strong a word, but it is lighthearted. I'll write as I would talk to you, as if we were sitting in your office together, chatting about a project, looking at work products, planning interactions with an executive, considering the reactions of managers or job incumbents, wondering if we can make a case based on talking to seven people instead of seventy.

◆ ◆ ◆

Performance analysis is your interface with the organization. It's the systematic way that performance professionals understand opportunities and problems and extend themselves into the organization and the field. It's relationships, questions, data, dissection, conversation, synthesis, collaboration, and marketing. It's a systematic strategy for figuring out what to do in a speedy fashion. It's an essential tool for coping and thriving now.

CHAPTER TWO

WHAT CAN WE DO FIRST AND FAST?

Paula: I want to understand what's going on before I start on this project. Maybe I'll do one of those whatchamacallits, a performance analysis, but I have hardly any time and not too much experience either.

Fritz: I know what you mean. People say we should do analysis, especially now that we're part of this performance improvement unit, but . . .

Paula: What should we do first? How are we supposed to do one? Where do we start? And time is always a concern.

Speedy Performance Analysis

Paula and Fritz probably have concerns similar to yours. What can they do first and fast? We call it performance analysis. How does it fit into the job? How is it done well? How is it done quickly? How is it done in a way that demonstrates immediate and tangible value to the organization? Just this morning, a former student now working at a telecommunications company admitted, "You know I believe in this analysis stuff, but my manager wants product, product, product. If there's a way I can do it really fast, so that maybe management doesn't even notice I'm doing it . . ." Another associate who works at a consulting firm noted, "Sometimes I think that my clients are more interested in getting something— anything—done than in getting it just right."

These perceptions are typical. Usually, there is little or no enthusiasm for analysis prior to action. Only occasionally will you hear,

> "Whatever it takes to get inside the heads of the engineers, do that. That will give us a good sense of how to proceed."
> "I want a solid study done before we jump into anything."
> "Take some time to get a clear picture of the situation. Get back to me with your recommendations."

In this book, we attempt to get around the lack of appreciation for study prior to action by using an approach that admits to not studying everything or everyone in meticulous detail. Our purpose isn't to know for sure but to describe and sketch, to provide fresh views, and to ask questions that push the project in practical and systemic, not habitual, directions. The beauty of this approach to performance analysis is that it helps you perform when you confront scant time and organizational support. Thus this book will help you fulfill your three purposes: (1) conducting performance analysis, (2) doing it well, and (3) doing it fast.

Performance Analysis in Context

Performance analysis is critical because performance is what matters in every organization. When results demand attention, human resources and training professionals turn from habitually favored interventions like training or facilitation to solutions tailored to the customer and situation. Even though snug interventions, like training, continue to be possible, even likely, solutions, no particular approach is guaranteed. Performance analysis is the study done to define solutions that go beyond the automatic to create fresh, data-driven, and coordinated approaches for customers and clients.

The job now is providing customized services with visible, measurable links to performance outcomes. With increased focus on the customer's strategic goals and the contexts in which they are attempting to achieve them, more professionals are finding their perspectives and even their physical locations shifting away from headquarters and out to the line units, often in far-flung settings. What training and human resources professionals do when they get there is seek to understand what's really going on in order to add value to the effort. They do that through performance analysis.

Defining Performance Analysis

Performance analysis (PA) is partnering with clients and customers to help them define and achieve their goals. PA involves reaching out for several perspectives on a problem or opportunity, determining any and all drivers toward or barriers to successful performance, and proposing a solution system based on what is learned, not on what is typically done.

Let's look at each component of the definition.

Partnering

In the past, a sure sign of success in our business was a grand training edifice. Many times over the past two decades, my first visit to a company would leave me stunned by the size and aesthetics of the training center. When I commented on the lush wood, furniture, rugs, and setting at one corporate training center, a director explained that the beauty was necessary to lure executives and managers from the operating units in to headquarters.

Often the problem that consumes human resources and training professionals is how to get *them* to come and partake of *what we know they need.* This reflects an old way of thinking. It's them and us, and it shouldn't be. Healthy human resources units are aggressively directing their perspectives and services at the needs of line organizations so that success parallels the priorities of the line organizations, not marketing schemes for training.

Partnership comes in many forms: through the physical placement of people in the field in permanent or itinerant roles; in the use of HR and training advisory committees composed of line managers; in cross-functional process action teams assembled to solve particular problems; and in assignment of individuals to develop specialized knowledge about the business and concerns of particular line units, even while these individuals still reside in centralized HR or training. A final and extreme possibility is to blow up the centralized entity and permanently house performance professionals closer to where the work gets done, perhaps with "dotted-line" relationships to a stripped-down central unit.

Take a moment to assess your progress on partnering in Exhibit 2.1. Where do you stand with a particular line unit that you and your group are charged with serving? How much of a partner are you today? For each item, give yourself a score from 0 to 10, with 10 representing strong agreement and 0 representing no truth at all in the statement for you. Then total your scores.

A perfect partnering score is 110. How close did you get? Are you satisfied? Would your customers and clients give you similar ratings? Would they express satisfaction with you as their partner? Can you use these items to stimulate discussion?

Goals

The goals that count are those of the organization and unit. Too often and not at all surprising, what has driven HR professionals has been our measurements or those of the central unit, indicators that may not immediately or blatantly contribute to organizational strategy. The best example is measuring viability using the proverbial "butts in seats." What that does is encourage training and HR professionals to become masters of marketing their products and services. Few customers would cheer for that goal.

EXHIBIT 2.1. PROGRESS ON PARTNERING SELF-ASSESSMENT.

_____	I consider myself knowledgeable about their business.
_____	I'm as comfortable in the field as I am at headquarters.
_____	Many people in the line unit know me and my work.
_____	When a new technology or perspective or product is on the horizon, I get involved early and often in the decision making.
_____	I know what it is that is of concern to line managers right now.
_____	I know what it is that is likely to emerge as a concern for line managers in the next year or two.
_____	When line managers have a problem, they ask my opinions.
_____	I get invited to informal and social events in the field.
_____	When I talk about the unit, I naturally use the word "we," because that's how I perceive our relationship.
_____	My colleagues in the field can describe what I do with and for them.
_____	If they had to pay for the work I do for them, the business unit would be willing to do so.

On the other hand, performance analysis directs attention to the customer's goals. Often this involves working with customers to clarify, define, and make concrete the directions in which they want to go. That might entail reviewing relevant policies, scanning the literature, and interviewing internal and external subject matter experts. Although there are other rich sources that describe excellent performance in detail, such as benchmarking reports and observations of master performers, they are time-consuming, and we're focusing performance analysis on those methods that can be carried out quickly.

Customers will usually appreciate the clarity and independence that a performance analyst provides. Century 21 International serves as an example (Strayer & Rossett, 1994). The real estate corporation sought a major training program for new sales associates. The request was for "twenty-one training modules in a variety of media." Rather than jumping into production mode, we focused instead on what the company *really* needed, soliciting the perspectives of regional directors, sales experts, brokers, and sales associates. This brought us to a wider and more systemic set of goals than originally conceived by the organization—and to a very different set of solutions. In addition to goals associated with listing, servicing, finance, and the like, we added a new position, the coach, and new perspectives and priorities for the organization.

Several Perspectives

The practice of performance analysis shakes you out of your shoes and into those of others in the organization. This shift is desirable because it enables you to see things in fresh and complex ways and to provide that more vivid view to customers. This becomes particularly important when you are constructing programs for dissemination in Indiana, Frankfurt, and Beijing.

A study for a medical manufacturing company provides an example. The executives wanted to know what training to do to help technical supervisors and managers grow in their jobs. By asking some hard questions about drivers and barriers, we were able to find out what training needed to be done and to detail significant cultural aspects that had gone awry. Quotes and anecdotes from the technical managers were compelling data and were used to "sell" management on a solution system instead of just a class on "effective meetings" or "negotiating."

There are many possible sources that you might tap during a performance analysis. They come in animate and inanimate forms. Human sources are executives, managers, supervisors, job incumbents, customers, experts, and colleagues. Inanimate sources are policies, records, tests, exit interviews, work products, reports, printouts, course materials, and performance appraisals. It would be unusual to use all these sources in any one performance analysis. The trick is to pick well and to recover from poor selections rapidly.

Here's an example of picking well. Some colleagues had developed new-product training for a bank. They thought they had created a nifty class for tellers and had that opinion confirmed through course reaction feedback after the sessions. "They loved it," crowed the instructional designers.

Unfortunately, they spoke too soon. A customer and performance focus necessitates waiting for business results before taking bows. On that measure, which in this case was defined as selling more of that particular financial product, things looked dismal a few months later. Soon, a director called to demand retraining. The professionals wisely demurred, pressing to take a look at *why* tellers weren't selling the product, rather than automatically scheduling more training.

Because the director was clamoring for action, they decided to schedule a morning of meetings with tellers and branch managers randomly pulled from different branches. The purpose was to find out why tellers weren't selling the account. It was possible that the tellers didn't "get" the new account and thus needed more training, but there were other possibilities as well. After the first meeting, a session with tellers, the reason was revealed. A subsequent meeting with other tellers and a group of managers confirmed the cause and provided additional numbers and quotes to use in making the case to the executives. The source of the problem was the incentive system. Branch managers and assistants were measured by wait time during peak times in the branches. Moving people through the line was what garnered supervisory praise and favors, not engaging customers in the more time-consuming relationship selling. Retraining wouldn't make any dent in the problem. Management needed to decide what it wanted most, sales or short lines at peak times.

We aren't always so fortunate as these professionals were in getting to the heart of the problem quickly. You will inevitably find yourself with a weak source, a particular threat when you are under severe time constraints. I had this problem during the launch of a management development effort. We were using performance analysis to swiftly scope the situation. We'd been directed to a technical manager who was touted as articulate, reflective about management, and able to talk about theory in light of what transpired on the manufacturing floor. But he couldn't, or he wouldn't with me. He had recently attended a scientific management conference and was chock full of buzzwords. Specific questions elicited glittering generalities. After about fifteen minutes, we parted. Other sources would be more fertile at this point, when time was of the essence. In fact, we found that judiciously selected literature on management development served as an excellent and substantive starting point for structuring interactions with managers. Most of the management sources, technical experts all, were better at reacting to proffered descriptions and examples than they were at generating descriptions themselves.

Problems and Opportunities

This book provides investigative tools for four typical situations, each of which is treated in detail in Chapter Four:

1. *Opportunities,* such as a new technology rollout or an effort to encourage contracts administrators to be empowered to make more decisions without turning to the legal department
2. *Problems,* such as missed sales expectations or increases in complaints about customer service or defective parts
3. *Development* of a group of people—for example, engineers, hospital administrators, or bank tellers
4. *Strategic planning,* which occurs when an executive wants assistance in looking at the situation in the midst of a changing competitive environment

Why these situations? Most often, customer and clients present them to us. These requests, both sophisticated and naive, are typical grist for the HR and training professional.

Sometimes, however, customers and clients don't ask for anything at all. Amanda Scott of IBM Education and Training has described to me the fertile possibilities presented by being proactive and conversant with the client, by not hanging about to wait for requests for help. If you're in a partnering relationship with the line, you're then in a position to anticipate an opportunity, note a problem, and collaborate on solutions. Katie Smith, formerly the practice leader for instructional systems design at Amoco and now a sales training manager at Eli Lilly, described the role that some organizational developers play at Amoco.

Assigned to particular business units, they continuously conduct *virtual* performance analyses, gathering data in formal and informal ways and passing off opportunities to human resources colleagues. Sensing, scoping, and relating *in advance of a request* prepare you for the times when customers present needs and opportunities.

Drivers and Barriers

Drivers and barriers are the levers in an organization that encourage, maintain, or impede performance. Although we discuss them in great detail in subsequent chapters, particularly in Chapter Three, a few examples might serve here. Skills are drivers. Access to information is a driver, just as the lack of it could deter performance. Another driver or barrier is the organizational culture, as it either encourages or discourages ways of behaving. The emphasis on drivers and barriers, current and anticipated, is what distinguishes performance analysis from other planning efforts. HR professionals have always worked with colleagues to establish *directions* through task analysis and strategic planning, for example. What's new and critical in performance analysis is targeting the causes of performance improvement, maintenance, *and* deterioration, thereby enabling the professional to tailor solutions to these circumstances. Then we can unleash the power of training needs assessment and an array of sibling HR interventions.

Ideally, the nature of the drivers and barriers define the services that we propose to provide to customers. We are thus more responsive than if we are doing something because we always have or because we were asked to.

Remember the financial product example presented earlier? The initial response to that request for assistance was the opposite of what we're talking about. The bank director said something like this to the instructional designers: "We want a class, something short and snappy. We want them to be able to quickly sell this fairly complicated new account." And that's what the instructional designers delivered.

But it didn't work. The reason? The professionals made no inquiries about barriers and drivers. They failed to ask about branch culture, about what mattered in the branches and what might get in the way of the desired sales performance. If they had, both a class and changes in incentives and policies would have taken place. Together, the class and the related changes compose a solution system.

Solution Systems

Solution systems are *integrated, cross-functional approaches to solving problems and realizing opportunities.* Driven by the nature of the drivers and barriers, interventions are tailored to the situation and coordinated across the organization. A typical solution system involves strategies that develop individual capacity and motivation, such as training and coaching, and organizational readiness and culture, such as recognition programs, workplace technology, and policies.

Consider something you do well and often at work. Why do you do it? There are probably many reasons: you can; you know how to; you want to; when you do it, you get recognized for it; you have the necessary tools and materials; doing it is important in the organization; the boss or your beloved makes a fuss about it; you perceive yourself as good at it . . . How long would you persist, if your manager and measurements paid it little mind?

The point is that performance happens for many reasons. And when it doesn't happen, that too is usually for several reasons. An example might be dieting. Why don't people enjoy successes in that area? There are many possible reasons: they don't want to; they don't know how to; they love food and the socializing it affords; they don't have low-calorie foods in the house; they are injured and can't exercise; they live with somebody who loves to eat, and they love to eat right along with him or her. If they committed themselves to dieting and hoped for significant and long-term improvements in weight control, they would need a solution system. That solution system would probably involve several approaches, including instruction, exercise, food choices, cupboard purging, negotiating with a partner, and coaching for confidence.

Let's try another example, one that is likely to be closer to the work that you do. Imagine that you had been asked to provide some leadership in your organization on the topic of sexual harassment. Although the executive that requested the assistance indicated preference for a "powerful class," performance analysis swiftly revealed that no class on earth, in and of itself, could accomplish such complex and important outcomes. A solution system was essential, likely involving executive stewardship; new policies regarding appraisal, recognition, and promotions; selection; training; and perhaps community internships. Performance analysis provides data that bolster your intuition about the value of a solution system and can enable you to sell such a "full-court press."

Even though solution systems make all the sense in the world, that doesn't mean they are easy to turn into a reality. A 1996 study that Carl Czech of SAIC and I completed and published in *Performance Improvement Quarterly* (Rossett & Czech, 1996) made the point: professionals trained in analysis and solution systems are often thwarted in their efforts because so many leaders prefer a silver bullet approach.

A solution system is the opposite of a silver bullet. Terry Bickham of the U.S. Coast Guard and I discovered this when we looked at diversity programs for law enforcement agencies. Often, the preference was for a class or a speaker or a human relations counselor. Leadership wanted to do *one thing*, preferably one self-contained and laudable event. But most complex changes in people and organizations involve coordinated and significant solution systems executed consistently over time.

Performance analysis provides a picture of what the linked interventions ought to be. They won't happen, however, if the professional hasn't established relationships that build trust and respect, facilitating cross-functional efforts.

Exhibit 2.2 is a self-check that will provide some indication of your likelihood to turn the results of your performance analysis into solution systems.

If your organization does not currently support these systemic approaches, be comforted by the fact that they are happening in a few places and could well be in your future. For example, Amoco established the Organizational Capability Group, which encompasses training, diversity, organizational effectiveness, and organizational development.

EXHIBIT 2.2. SOLUTION SYSTEM SELF-CHECK.

_____ I am familiar with other performance-enhancing interventions, such as organizational development, job redesign, and reengineering.

_____ I know the people in the organization and outside who have expertise in these sibling HR interventions.

_____ I feel comfortable working with peers with expertise in other interventions.

_____ I can point to projects in which I've linked my work with the work of colleagues from other interventions.

_____ I can describe the results of systemic approaches in ways that will resonate for my customers.

_____ I know how to explain the relationship between performance analysis and solution systems.

_____ My manager encourages me to broker solution systems and to involve other units in our projects.

_____ My manager smooths the way for collaborations across organizational boundaries.

_____ The performance measurements in my organization encourage me to work with colleagues in sibling performance-enhancing units.

_____ The performance measurements in the organization encourage my colleagues to contribute to cross-functional solution systems.

AT&T Universal Card Services has established a similar structure to facilitate collaboration across service units, a unique effort to expand the role of human resources and training professionals. Andersen Consulting's Change Management Services, a conglomerate composed of professionals representing many of the traditional human resources and information technology domains, is driven by the desire to facilitate the establishment of successful solution systems for clients. There are more examples, suggesting that big companies are making organizational changes to overcome some of the daunting aspects of solution systems.

So Many Analyses, So Little Time

Performance analysis. Front-end analysis. Task analysis. Content analysis. Learner analysis. Context analysis. Root cause analysis. We could devote a book to the distinctions drawn between these concepts. But this isn't that book. Why?

Making those distinctions isn't necessary for effective practice—and this book is about practice. We'll focus on the kinds of information and sources that you need to tap right up front, when you are launching an effort, in order to consult effectively with clients and customers, no matter what you dub the analysis. The best place for defining these terms is in a lengthier text or a glossary. (You can refer to the Glossary at the end of this book.)

Now that I've convinced you that the fine distinctions aren't important, I'm going to revisit the distinction made earlier between performance analysis and training needs assessment. That's one that is important, because both combine to provide services in the organization.

Too often, admittedly, needs assessments are appreciated more in theory than in practice. Too often, lamentably, I hear, "They just won't give me time to do a needs assessment."

In reaction to that, and after observing some nifty practices in organizations like IBM, Amoco, Wells Fargo, and SBC, I've cut the front end into manageable bite sizes. One bite is performance analysis. The other and usually lengthier munch is what some call needs assessment and others call training needs assessment.

Performance analysis provides preliminary study of the situation in order to determine if and when a more detailed training needs assessment is warranted.

Training needs assessment is study to design and develop instructional and informational programs and materials, after the performance analysis has determined that training or informational materials are indeed appropriate. The needs assessments involve subject matter study, audience analysis, determination of prerequisite skills and attitudes, error and work product examination, resolution of disagreements among experts, and definition of the lion's share of the details that will congeal in the instructional and informational approaches. We invest in needs assessments only after we are certain that education, training, or information can be critical factors in solving the problem or realizing the opportunity. Thus, input for a needs assessment comes from performance analysis.

Performance analysis is what happens up front and immediately, prior to needs assessment. It is the expeditious study that enables you to determine the general nature of the drivers and barriers and thus the related solution system. Performance assessment asks, Why aren't they doing it? What might get in the way if we make these changes? Will training be involved? Will documentation? What about job redesign? Process reengineering? New policies and incentives? Programs for managers and executives? What's it going to take?

There are similarities between performance analysis and training needs assessment. They both represent methods for figuring out what to do. They are efforts to understand and serve customers. And they rely on sources for data. They seek the same kinds of information but at different levels of detail. The difference lies in where they are in the food chain, so to speak, as represented in Figure 2.1.

Performance analysis is what you do first and fast. Training needs assessment is what you do to create the tangible solution(s) to the problem or opportunity. Whereas performance analysis is that first response, needs assessment is the more measured and production-oriented effort, something I've described in detail in my book *Training Needs Assessment.* Performance analysis helps you determine what to

FIGURE 2.1. PA TO TNA.

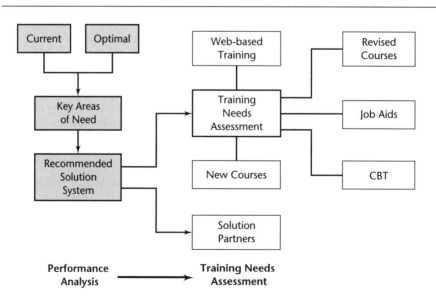

recommend. If training or information or references are indicated, then training needs assessment enables that recommendation to become a focused program.

Performance analysis identifies the people in an organization who must come to the table to develop and coordinate the solution system. It is the first portion of the services provided to customers and clients. The people doing needs assessment receive a hand-off from the performance analysts, perhaps a report or a briefing detailing those aspects of the effort amenable to training and information solutions. It is this PA document that will sell and justify the time and expense of meetings with subject matter experts and practitioners, and the lengthier examination of the literature and work products, so often a part of the needs assessment (detailed in *Training Needs Assessment*).

Jim Marshall of the Lightspan Partnership Inc. noted that needs assessment sometimes feels self-serving. "Typically, training professionals do needs assessments knowing that we're going to go forward and build some training. We say that's not the case, but it's hard to find an example of a training person eschewing the opportunity to develop a training program, and the new media make it even harder to resist."

The seductive nature of the new media is another good reason to add performance analysis right up front. Performance analysis keeps the focus on the customers and their purposes. The goal is to find the "right" bundle of interventions.

◆ ◆ ◆

In this chapter we've described the challenges confronting training and human resources professionals:

Intensified performance orientation—habitual solutions aren't sufficient

Expectations regarding consultation services delivered to customers and clients

Increased emphasis on understanding customer needs

Increased accountability for demonstrating value to
clients and customers

Limited time and support for analysis

More study prior to choosing a solution

We've also focused on definitions, particularly looking at performance analysis and then comparing it with training needs assessment. What is performance analysis? Performance analysis

Enables you to reach out and understand the organization

Establishes partnerships with customers and clients and sibling colleagues, such as process reengineers and organizational effectiveness experts

Relies on many sources of information, including experts, managers, associates, records, and work products

Produces a picture of what's encouraging or blocking performance in the organization and what must be done about it

Sets the table for needs assessment

Generates solution systems

Does all this swiftly, because performance analysis is a springboard to organizational partners who will then contribute to the effort

Performance analysis helps you determine what to recommend. If training or information or references are indicated, then training needs assessment enables that recommendation to come to fruition.

CHAPTER THREE

PERFORMANCE ANALYSIS BASICS

Andy: I've been doing analysis for what feels like years. But I've got my doubts about how much difference it's making. One customer even said the dreaded words "analysis-paralysis."

Marcus: I know what you mean. I believe in study before action, of course, but I'm concerned that my study isn't as sharp as it could be. And I have trouble selling it to my customers.

Beth: The trick is clarity. I think we've been stumbling around. Maybe we need to both tighten and speed up our focus.

In this chapter, we'll go to the heart of the matter: we'll talk about the basic principles of performance analysis and about the kinds of information we seek and the sources of that information.

Principles of Performance Analysis

Five assumptions drive performance analysis:

1. Study prior to action improves the quality of the effort and the results.

2. Incorporation of several sources yields a better program than an approach that relies only on the perspectives of one source (such as an executive or an expert) or even of the executive and the human resources professional together.
3. Data, broadly defined, are critical to figuring out what to do.
4. A systematic approach to analysis is good for the organization and its people.
5. A systemic approach to solutions is good for the organization and its people.

Let's look at each of these assumptions.

Study prior to action improves quality and results. Is there any question that a reflective examination of the possibilities and the current situation will yield a superior effort? The quality movement has firmly ingrained the value of study and measurement in American organizations. However, a frequent obstacle to analysis is customers' unwillingness to invest time and energy in study that precedes events and programming. Most line managers want what they want when they want it. They want it now, not later, and certainly not after a study has been completed. The beauty of performance analysis, as conceptualized here, is that it assumes scant time and organizational support yet bases decisions on more solid footings. We're trying to improve what we can do within the constraints of that enduring preference for a quick fix.

Incorporation of several sources yields a better program than an approach that relies only on the perspectives of one source (such as an executive or an expert) or even of the executive and the human resources professional together. The quest for information from several sources is an effort to achieve "triangulation." Triangulation increases our confidence about a finding by helping us determine if other sources echo it. Matthew Miles and Michael Huberman (1984), authorities on qualitative research, note that we should draw comfort from the work of detectives who use a *modus operandi* approach, amassing alibis, fingerprints, hair samples, accounts, opinions, and the like, in order to draw conclusions about a case. We're attempting to do pretty much the same thing as we seek the perspectives of several sources on the same topic in order to come to more sturdy conclusions. We'll also profit from the politics of inclusion, as we go beyond the executive and expert to solicit involvement from other regions and countries and from the people closest to the work. Experience suggests that people are more likely to support a solution that they or an associate had a role in defining. A final benefit is that participation in the up-front study is a form of education for participants.

A leader in an insurance company issued this request: "Transform our organization so that our people are doing things in teams. I understand this here is a really fine multimedia program. Buy it, schedule it, whatever. Let's get the transition happening." It's almost laughable to imagine that any single set of materials in any medium could achieve this large and complex goal—yet the executive was licking his lips over just that idea. And he is not alone. Bringing teaming, or just about any critical change to an organization, involves eschewing silver bullets, *listening* to many sources of information, and then birthing a solution system. No question, it takes a village to improve performance. Performance analysis helps define who will live and work in that village.

Data, broadly defined, are critical to figuring out what to do. Data are what we gather from sources. They include facts, attitudes, opinions, and actions that turn into information when we organize and infuse them with meaning. Data are thus the basis for the assumptions that we cobble together to make inferences and derive conclusions. We collect formal and informal data to make certain that history or whim or habit or politics or metrics isn't pressing us toward recommendations or actions not indicated by the realities of the work, the worker, and the workplace.

During performance analysis, we want to define data broadly, including, for example, letters of complaint and praise from customers, wait time and response rates, conversations enjoyed in the lunch line, employee opinions solicited via climate surveys, mission statements, elevator chats, interviews with randomly pulled supervisors, and focus groups composed of model performers. Just this morning I examined formal data gathered during performance modeling sessions with financial analysts for a computer company. What resulted from their group meetings was a first-cut picture of the common goals, skills, and knowledge of the financial analyst. Soon, individual interviews with supervisors and employees will capture data about priorities and perceptions regarding obstacles and barriers. Another data source is the priorities of the two executives most concerned about the productivity and morale of the financial people. Each piece of the data can be thought of as a piece of a jigsaw puzzle, in this case a puzzle focused on the work life of a new financial analyst for a global technology company. The small data elements eventually fit together into a more complete and textured picture of the situation.

A systematic approach to analysis is good for the organization and its people. Performance analysis is systematic: it has defined purpose, components, data, input, transactions, and output. It is standardized and repeatable. Of critical importance is that the output from one phase of the effort serves as input for subsequent efforts, enlightening decision making as you move toward a recommendation. Performance analysis serves here as the first aspect of the system; data from this effort enlighten training needs assessment and the messages conveyed to other professionals who might contribute to the challenge.

It is nothing new to think about the work of the human resources professional as a systematic endeavor. Since World War II, based on lessons from Robert Gagne and others, professionals have attempted to use data to identify objectives and then, based on the nature of the objectives, to craft strategies and evaluation items.

Table 3.1 expands on the description of performance analysis as a systematic activity.

A systemic approach to solutions is good for the organization and its people. The results of performance analysis respect the fact that performance occurs within a system. No matter the power of a course or the rightness of the selection of a person for a job, continued excellent performance depends on the integrated elements that wrap around people—on the performance *system*, which comprises standards, feedback, knowledge, incentives, recognition, information, management, sponsorship, technology, tools, processes, and more.

Performance analysis provides the details about what is and isn't working within the current system and about what needs to be included in the system to come. Thus, how an organization defines the services and products to be provided to customers and clients comes from rec-

TABLE 3.1. PERFORMANCE ANALYSIS IS A SYSTEMATIC EFFORT.

Purpose	The purpose of performance analysis is to help the organization accomplish its goals by incorporating data from varied sources and making effective decisions or recommendations about what should happen next.
Components	The components of performance analysis are sources, kinds of information, data, data-gathering strategies, and solution systems.
Data	The recommendations that result from performance analysis are driven by the data that is gathered from sources, not by whim, politics, or historical precedent.
Defined input, trans-actions, and output	*Input* is sources' perspectives on the work, worker, and work-place. Examples of input are interviews, records, and work products. Performance analysis *transactions* are the methods used to gather information, such as interviews, review of records and the literature, and focus groups. The output of performance analysis is twofold: first, the recommendation regarding what to do and the partners that need to collaborate to do it; second, the involvement and goodwill generated by asking sources to participate in the process.
Output from one phase serves as input for the next	Each contact with a source influences subsequent contacts. For example, what we learn from one expert will influence the way we structure interviews with job incumbents. The information provided by work products helps target the questions we ask about what might be driving the problem.

ognizing that information about drivers and causes must define what to do, not customer habit or human resources department metrics, as is so often the case. Table 3.2 describes the elements of a systemic approach.

Jeanne Strayer and I (1994) described an exemplary program for Century 21 International in *Performance Improvement Quarterly*. New sales associates were the challenge. Fresh from licensing classes and certification tests, many new associates soon became discouraged as they attempted to make sales and failed repeatedly. Not surprising, they often quit, creating problems for themselves and the company. After a *systematic* analysis, the company chose a *systemic* approach to solving the problem. This approach involved selection of the "right" coaches, training for coaches, shared training materials for coaches and new sales people, and monetary incentives for coaches. The simple and typical thing—training modules for the sales associates—would not have made a dent

TABLE 3.2. PERFORMANCE ANALYSIS YIELDS SYSTEMIC RECOMMENDATIONS.

Focuses on components and relationships of an entity	Rather than looking at components in isolation, performance analysis looks at the relationships between the entities in an organization. For example, a systemic approach to improved customer service would acknowledge the many organizational and individual levers that must work together to accomplish the business result.
Elements influence each other	Consider the customer service example. Altering the job descriptions and training for supervisors will influence the performance of service representatives and their immediate needs for information and development.
Seeks and addresses root causes	Performance analysis attempts to find and solve underlying problems, not just their symptoms. In the customer service example, the PA might trace the problem of customer complaints to poor service as a result of high employee turnover, which is due in turn to a combination of a poorly structured incentive system and outdated tools plus a rapidly changing product database that leaves employees feeling insecure about their ability to help customers.
Acknowledges distinctions between means and ends	Customers say, "We need a coach out there, somebody patient at working with people who are afraid of technology." This is a *means* statement. Although this *might* be the best way to deal with the challenge, we want to focus first on the factors that influence the desired outcomes, rather than do the automatic or habitual thing.
Emphasizes solution systems predicated on causes, barriers, drivers	Performance analysis works on the principle that complex problems typically require multiple, rather than single, solutions. For example, redesigning both the incentives and the tools, often in conjunction with some training, would be likely to produce better results than training without related organizational interventions.

in the numbers. The performance analysis provided the data needed to sell the more complicated, cross-functional system to management.

Kinds of Information

During performance analysis, we seek two broad kinds of information that serve as umbrellas for many concerns and considerations. First, we seek the performance and perspectives that the organization and its leaders are trying to put in place. Let's call them *directions*. Two kinds of information influence our quest for directions: information about "optimals" and information about "actuals" (the status quo). We derive directions from perspectives on exemplary or optimal performance and from current or actual performance. Some examples of optimals are what expert sales people know that enables them to qualify customers, or what a fine chef does to make a plate look tempting, or what a master mechanic thinks about when looking at a computer printout associated with an airplane. Some examples of actuals are error rates, help desk inquiries, and retail returns.

We also seek information about performance *drivers*, the factors that are now blocking or aiding performance or those that might do so in the future. *Causes, barriers,* and *obstacles* are synonyms. Typical drivers are skills, motivation, incentives, tools, and work processes. If you think about it, you can see that all of them are involved in ensuring performance. For example, even if you know about performance analysis from this book or wherever, you're far more likely to do it if you think it's important; are encouraged by your manager and prodded by a line on your performance appraisal; get applauded for it by colleagues; and are provided some technology support in a pinch. The "knowing about it" part is necessary, certainly, but not sufficient.

Let's set up another example of drivers. Your organization commits itself to the shift from training to performance. They write about it in job descriptions and standards. They communicate about it through a marketing program for internal and external customers. They alter the incentives to reflect the shift. And supervisors begin urging training and development professionals to predicate decisions on performance analysis. Will this organization shift successfully? Maybe. I can't tell without data from an analysis. But experience with this mission in several organizations suggests that the solution system just described is ignoring two drivers. First, organizations must develop their people so that they know how to fluently do the things involved in the transition. Second, the organization must tend to turf issues in a way that will encourage collaborative solutions across units.

Let's look at another example. Consider the people who screen us and our carry-on baggage at airports. What are their likely drivers?

What are the components of a system that would strengthen and maintain their performance? Certainly, they need to know what to look for, how to screen, how to decipher the computer screens, how to approach passengers, and how to do it all swiftly. They also need to know why their efforts are important and to care enough to maintain effort and performance in a job that is repetitive and unexciting. Yet another factor is technology; it seems obvious that better scanners are critical for doing this job. Finally, these people need to believe that there are incentives for attentiveness. They must know that their performance will be tested, and that feedback, supervision, and ramifications are certain.

Whereas the quest for directions sketches out the scope of the effort, the analysis of drivers determines what needs to be done to successfully develop performance, people, and the organization.

Anyone familiar with my work is noting that I've boiled the effort down from a longer list of kinds of information to two. From a quest for information about optimals, actuals, barriers, feelings, and solutions detailed in Rossett (1987), I'm advising an early emphasis on directions and drivers. The discussion that follows shows how I've streamlined the effort.

We'll examine directions and drivers here, focusing on methods and sources most likely to contribute to capturing them, furthering our goals of both quality *and* speed.

Directions

Directions set the course for the effort. The task during performance analysis is to determine, from the perspective of judiciously selected sources, what people ought to be doing and considering. Optimals are what we want the people to know and do and what the conditions are in which they will be doing them. Actuals detail the current situation.

There are two ways we get at directions for the effort. The first is focused, positive, and prospective. Here are some questions for the customer or sponsor who has initiated the effort:

What are you attempting to accomplish? Why?

Can you describe some of the changes and improvement you'd like to see?

Will effort in other regions or countries be different? How so?

Do you have any documents or policies that explain what it is that job incumbents ought to be doing and why it's so important?

Who in the organization must be involved as we move forward on this?

Are there any examples of model work products to which you can direct us?

What experts are essential to involve in this effort?

What do you think that your more effective people know and refer to that others perhaps don't?

Are you or colleagues reading anything that has been particularly influential?

What are the challenges that they will be confronting?

How is the work environment going to shift in ways that matter to [this topic or group of people]?

Another tack on optimals is to approach them from the current situation—the actuals. Look for information about which current efforts the sponsor seeks to maintain or increase and where the problems are. The opposite of the problems provides insight into where efforts ought to be focused and where questions about drivers will eventually be focused.

Consider the case of a performance professional who has been asked to do something to improve the writing of engineers. The sponsor suggested that a course might be a good idea, but she is leaving it up to her performance consultant. How to approach this? The more time-consuming option is to commence with questions about the essence of good writing for engineers. This sounds like the beginning of a lengthy study. Wouldn't it be better to begin by finding out where the engineers have been messing up, from the perspective of the sponsor and the clients who raised the issue? That's using the status quo to provide direction and ensure an authentic focus. Here are some questions that could be used with the sponsor and others that she designates: Why are you particularly concerned about their writing now? What's bad about their writing? I asked you to gather some writing samples that were particularly problematic; can you show me where the problems are? Can you randomly pull some examples of their writing and show me instances of the most vexing problems? Do they submit the writing products on time? About what are customers complaining? Is there anything you like about the writing they've done?

Here are some additional sample questions that use current successes and failures to frame the effort and point toward desired directions:

> Is anybody here doing it, already talking about it and thinking about it as you wish others would? What about their approaches attracts you, strikes you as model? Is there anything that they are doing that you'd like to increase or change?
>
> As you consider the efforts going on around the globe, what strikes you as particularly useful? How can we learn from these efforts?
>
> Have there been any examples of flawed performance that concern you? What were the problems, as you see them?
>
> Are there any examples of flawed work products to which you can direct us? What's the problem with them?
>
> What questions do people have? What concerns? Complaints?
>
> How do employees currently handle the work in ways that would be desirable to maintain?
>
> Is there anything about what's going on now that has served as a stimulus for this initiative?
>
> What problems do the employees now solve that will continue to be important in the future? Any emerging problems or situations?

Here we're attempting to ascertain the focus of the effort, its general outline, the sweet spots and opportunities to make a difference, and then to identify if there are obvious and critical gaps between what's now happening and what ought to be happening.

The search for a general picture of optimals brings us to such sources as the initiator, selected plaudits and complaints gathered from customers, policies and job descriptions, model and flawed work products, and a favored expert who, best of all, has committed his or her ideas to print or electronic formats. More labor intensive sources of optimals, such as review of extensive documentation, attendance at vendor courses, lengthy interviews with subject matter experts, observation and interviews with model job performers, and substantive review of the published literature, are appropriate later, during training needs assessment, when resources have been committed to capturing and representing a *detailed* picture of optimals.

Tap as few live sources for optimals as possible. They are time-consuming and expensive. For example, if the problem is the writing skills of engineers, now is not the time to interview model engineer writers or even to review their excellent output. Far better during performance analysis to talk to the people who are complaining, see what is making them unhappy, look at examples of rotten reports, and examine current policies and standards for what is expected. Remember, during PA you're not creating the details of the solutions. Rather, you're figuring out what that solution ought to be and who needs to come to the table to build it. That takes us to the issue of drivers.

Drivers

Now we decide what it's going to take to realize the opportunity or solve the problem. We do this by asking sources for their perspectives on what's been getting in the way, what it will take to make it happen, or what will encourage or impede performance. In fact, it's a good idea to ask those very questions, and then to ask questions specifically associated with the four kinds of drivers I will be describing shortly.

The major purpose of performance analysis is to figure out what to do. During performance analysis, we emphasize the quest for drivers rather than the detailed definition of the domain or content area, because it is the drivers that define solutions.

Think about drivers as everything that it takes to enable performance to "grow." Just as flowers require consistent exposure to soil, nutrients, sun, and moisture, performance grows and blossoms in a similarly supportive system. Let's look at four kinds of drivers and then at interventions matched to them:

Skills, Knowledge, and Information. A successful performer knows how to do what is expected and when it is appropriate to do it. Let's start by focusing on knowing what's expected. Recently, Sheila Bobenhouse of SAIC in San Diego commented on a lesson learned early in her career. She had responsibility for a teller certification program in a financial institution. She believes the power of the certification program was in its published definition of teller standards and career path, even more than in its training or promotion opportunities.

The most familiar aspect of this driver is skill and knowledge. A synonym is *capacity,* the individual's ability to do what is needed, to know what he or she needs to know, to know where to search and find what's necessary, and to handle opportunities and challenges.

In the era of knowledge and mobile work, we've become more conscious of the importance of employees' understanding their work, not just their being able to do it robotically. The employees' comprehension of why they are doing their work and of its fit with other aspects of work contributes to their ability to handle the unforeseen and to do it in settings that aren't closely supervised. Robert Reich, President Clinton's former Secretary of Labor, emphasized this issue. He believes that technical training that is purely algorithmic and narrowly defined as how to do something necessitates the need for continuous retraining, an expense most organizations wish to avoid.

Another emergent aspect of this driver is information. Information is useful data that are available to employees but aren't necessarily committed to memory through the rigors of training. The data might be provided as documentation or job aids or a computer database. Examples are the Yellow Pages, guidance on how to change the message on voice mail, an automated program that prompts decisions regarding retirement investments, and the rich databases that the large consulting firms, such as Ernst and Young and Andersen Consulting, provide to their employees. These databases make data, information, knowledge, expertise, and wisdom more widely available. In his excellent book, *Intellectual Capital,* Thomas Stewart (1997, p. 63) described the wealth of intellect within the organization in this way: "The inevitable metaphor is the iceberg. Above the surface, the financial and physical resources. . . . Beneath, unseen, something vastly larger . . . but whose contours no one knows."

There are many ways to drive or encourage performance in an organization. After an analysis with the people doing or attempting the work, you then get to choose whether to invest in enhancing memory through training or to provide some form of information support. The solution is debatable. What's important for us here is that the dialogue occurs, with a rich array of options on the table.

Motivation. *Motivation* is a word that gets bandied about. Every leader wants motivated people. We're all familiar with employees we praise for being gung ho or castigate for being out to lunch. But what *is* motivation, and how can we use it to improve performance?

Motivation can be viewed as persistence of effort by people. A motivated teacher keeps offering up examples, calling parents, and providing feedback. A motivated customer service representative seeks the answer for the caller, even when he doesn't know it off the top of his head and his documentation in that area is out-of-date.

Why do some persist and others not? Two factors are typically given credit for motivation. The first is the individual's ability to name, list, and describe the reasons for doing this or that. This is the employee's awareness of the value of the topic or content. She knows why service is important, why answering questions matters, and how her efforts fit into the greater mission. Most important, she buys into all this, not because the boss or the instructor told her so or is hovering but because she shares commitment to the direction.

The second factor is the individual's confidence. This is can-do feeling. Imagine a customer service rep who feels competent regarding computers. He hears that the organization is moving documentation to automated databases that can be accessed during phone calls. No problem with motivating this representative on this aspect of the job.

The two motivation factors are related. They can enhance each other or cancel each other out. For example, consider the California regulation that all public school teachers must learn about computers in education to retain their credentials; soon, knowledge of computers will be required even to obtain those credentials. Teachers who see the value and feel confident are motivated. These early adapters attend classes, read about software and hardware for schools, and use what they glean. Some other teachers, however, aren't at all motivated. When they are queried, we find that most of their reluctance comes from problems of confidence. Even though they are aware of potential benefits for their classrooms, they don't perceive themselves as competent to employ technology. The absence of confidence undermines their motivation. Reiterating the benefits of computers won't bring these teachers to the computer table. The solution must match their driver, in this case, lack of confidence.

A pal of mine teaches mandated leadership classes for automotive supervisors. It's written into the union contract. They must be there. When my friend walks into class, he confronts significant motivation problems caused not by an absence of confidence in this case but by self-confidence. He's gone so far as to label them "hostile." Because these supervisors think that their skills are sufficient, even strong, they see little reason to be doing anything more to buff up. Table 3.3 illustrates this and other situations.

Because motivation has these two related components, questions during performance analysis must get at both. First, there are some overarching questions that you must ask of sponsors and eventually direct to the job incumbents themselves: Do employees share your

TABLE 3.3. EMPLOYEE MOTIVATION IN BRIEF.

	Aware of benefits	*Unconvinced of benefits*
Confident	"Gung ho"	"Hostile"
Not confident	"Timid"	"Out to lunch"

enthusiasm in this domain? Are they motivated? Do they appear eager to do this? To move in this direction?

Here are some questions about the *perceived benefits*: Why is this important? What's in it for the organization, the unit, the individuals? Do they know the reasons? Have they been informed?

And some questions regarding *confidence:* Are your people ready to move in this direction? Would you describe them as confident? What are their related skills and knowledge? Are they able at related things? Has anybody asked what they need in order to handle this?

During performance analysis, you parse motivation so that strategies can eventually be targeted to the particular situation. The perception of value and benefit is built by showing employees related, authentic problems that these skills will address. It is also useful to directly tell them why these skills are important. Finally, share data from the performance analysis or the literature documenting the need. Confidence is best built by setting up early, small successes; reminding employees of prior and related learning; sharing the testimonials of others who went from timidity to success; and describing the subsequent support system that will wrap around employees' efforts.

Environment, Tools, and Processes. Here we focus attention on organizational issues. Are the policies timely and supportive of the effort? Are the tools in place? Is there enough memory in the computers to use the software that people are being trained to employ and encouraged to adore? Are the databases up-to-date? Are jobs and processes set up to facilitate effort? Can employees find what they need to get the work done?

Historically, human resources professionals haven't paid sufficient attention to these crucial organizational questions, yet an infertile environment can block the success of even the most skilled and motivated individuals. A favorite example comes from a situation in which sales people were trained and exhorted to sell new high-end products when they had no budget to purchase them for demonstration. These salespeople were ready and eager, but they lacked the systems to show to potential customers. Another example was provided by a company that trained instructional design and delivery people in a multimedia authoring system. After a class on the authoring system, the designers returned to new, fast, and fabulous hardware and software. They devoted themselves to generating electronic lessons for delivery to PCs on the desktops of employees across their large organization. Unfortunately, rank-and-file desktop machines were several versions behind the equipment on which the courseware was generated. Oooops. The lessons looked bad, slow, and clunky to the people who counted, the users in the field. Good performance was decimated by a badly planned environment. When asked, the people in the field thought that the multimedia training was bad. Was it? We don't know, because the installed platform gave the training little chance to succeed.

Recently I wanted to reschedule a mammography at my HMO. I visited a booth just outside the door of my primary health care provider (a woman formerly known as my doctor). The scheduling booth looked friendly, with pictures of cute animals and smiley faces. And the woman in the booth, she too was friendly, obviously trained and exhorted to treat customers first. I saw an innocuous job aid to that effect tacked near the smiley faces.

Unfortunately, the woman who is the scheduler isn't authorized to schedule, not really, not without specific authorization. I'd had this treasured authorization document originally, when they scheduled and botched my first appointment a few months prior. Now, months later, this person couldn't find my permission in the computer, and she couldn't immediately put her hands on the hard copies of my files. Instead, she promised to get back to me later via telephone.

I walked away from the booth certain that she wouldn't get back to me. She didn't.

When I called a week later, after much button pushing and revisiting this boring story, somebody informed me that I did indeed have a scheduled mammography appointment. With just a little bit of annoyance, she wondered how I was going to diligently appear at my appointment if I didn't know about it. Good question. Do you see a few problems with job description, automated tools, policies, and processes?

Incentives. Together with the environment and policies described previously, incentives make up what many label as "culture." I heard Peter Senge of MIT, author of the *Fifth Discipline,* define culture as those aspects of the organization that are so ingrained that we no longer notice them. That definition is useful for us. The performance analyst investigates drivers so as to make such factors manifest and workable.

How does the organization tell the employee that something is important? Does the performance management system applaud effort in this domain? How? Where does related effort get recognized? Do people throughout the organization think that the leadership cares? Why? What tells employees that this is a top priority? How does the organization express priorities to the employee? Is there anything that the organization does to give a mixed message to employees?

One common problem is ignoring desired performance. When you ask a group of training professionals about the incentives for excellent performance, they'll often laugh. Too frequently, they perceive none. In fact, some contend that there is punishment associated with excellence, with the best people getting the thorniest clients or challenges.

Sometimes the organization punishes the very behavior that it works so hard to put in place. Performance improvement efforts provide a good example. All the management development in the world about how to do performance appraisals cannot compensate for a policy manual that devotes ten pages to how to submit a grievance and one and a half pages to the importance, value, and heroics associated with the appraisal process. Supervisors and managers swiftly figure out that sincere reviews could well cost them in time and aggravation. Where does the system encourage the bravery and priorities on which an effective appraisal system is predicated?

Another typical problem with incentives is when they conflict, or when the organization is rewarding behavior that crowds out the desired performance. This happens to customer service people who are often measured and applauded for the quantity of their contacts but exhorted to deliver high-quality, relationship- and loyalty-building interactions. The organization is speaking with two voices. The individual is likely to hear the one that is linked to performance-management metrics.

There are many perfectly reasonable ways to think about the topic of drivers or root causes or barriers. Thomas Gilbert (1978), Robert Mager and Peter Pipe (1984), and Dick Swanson (1994), for example, have done early and excellent work in this area. Table 3.4 presents one way of talking about the four kinds of drivers.

Using Drivers to Define Solutions

There is a superb reason for the quest for drivers: drivers define solutions. They tell us what we have to do now and next. If you know what's causing bad performance or driving successful efforts, you know what you need to do to change or maintain. Table 3.5 links drivers with an array of interventions.

TABLE 3.4. DRIVERS AND EXAMPLES.

Type of Driver	Examples
Skills, Knowledge, Information	Teachers leave their computers in the closet because they don't know how to use them.
	Contracts administrators resist making decisions because they don't know they are expected to.
	Service reps guess more than they ought because the documentation is out-of-date.
Motivation	Clerks don't see the value of the new software. The old one works just fine, in their view.
	Many teachers fear computers, noting that they're people-people, not techies.
Environment	The documentation and directories are housed way across the office and frequently misplaced.
	Personnel reenter a nine-digit code three different times during an order-fulfillment process.
	Managers don't approve of the approach that the organization is touting during training, and they make it known.
Incentives	Supervisors who rate employees as other than stellar are expected to fill out forms and attend meetings to justify these ratings.
	High-performing human resources professionals are assigned the most difficult clients.

TABLE 3.5. DRIVERS MATCHED WITH SOLUTIONS.

Type of Driver	Description	Solutions
Lack of skill, knowledge, or information	People don't . . . because they don't know how, or they've forgotten, or there's just too much to know.	Education, training Information support (job aids) Documentation, performance support Coaching, mentoring Clarity regarding standards Communications initiatives
Weak or absent motivation	People don't . . . because they don't care, don't see the benefits, or don't believe they can.	Education, training Information support (job aids) Documentation, performance support Coaching, mentoring Participatory goal setting Communications initiatives
Ineffective environment, tools, processes	People don't . . . because processes or jobs are poorly designed or because necessary tools are unavailable	Reengineered work processes New or improved tools or technologies or work spaces Job design or redesign Job enrichment Participatory decision making
Ineffective or absent incentives	People don't . . . because doing it isn't recognized, doing it is a hassle, or not doing it is ignored.	Improved appraisal and recognition programs Management development New policies New and shared goal setting

Let's look at an example. Imagine that the problem, in the view of key administrators, is the failure of professors to use multimedia in their university classes. The university has offered several classes over the past few semesters, and many professors have attended. In fact, attendees gave the workshops very good ratings. Still, the use rate shows only a slight uptick. The responsible administrator is thinking about more workshops. You convince her to let you take a quick look at the situation before scheduling more training. Here's what your study turns up, presented in Table 3.6. This example focuses on data from only one source, a randomly pulled group of professors from the larger population of those who had attended the multimedia workshops. Although talking with this group wouldn't constitute the entire PA, you can see why these professors would be its key players.

TABLE 3.6. DRIVERS MATCHED WITH SOLUTIONS: AN EXAMPLE.

Findings	Drivers	Potential Solutions
Professors (seven of ten) expressed doubts about the usefulness of multi-media. Half of interviewed profs agreed or strongly agreed with statement "Multimedia is more likely to add glitz to my class than substance."	Motivation (value) is a problem. Knowledge, too, is a problem, as they admit to not knowing how to make significant use of technology in their classes. None see the use of media as particularly core to their work.	Disseminate results of review of published literature regarding technology benefits for higher education teaching. Conduct workshop with rich examples of uses keyed to curriculum areas. Coach for lesson planning to assist profs as they attempt to integrate multimedia. Surround role model profs and their uses of multimedia with good publicity.
One prof (of ten) admitted to concern about how to operate the equipment.	Motivation (confidence) does not appear to be a problem. Skills and knowledge do not appear to be factors.	
CD-ROMs and players are available at a centralized unit, across the campus, and profs are unwilling to go fetch.	Environment is a hassle.	Make equipment and titles more widely available. Sprinkle available classrooms across the campus so that faculty can more easily plug and play. Co-locate titles at a central resource *and* at most relevant departments.
Three profs didn't know where the equipment resides and policies for use. Six of ten said they didn't know what titles were available.	Information is a problem.	Establish libraries of titles associated with the colleges, their computer labs, and their academic disciplines, instead of having a campuswide collection. Place information on-line. When new titles are purchased, regularly inform faculty in associated disciplines. Provide small grant programs for faculty to purchase titles that support their lessons and priorities. In return, ask them to describe uses in a database that is widely available.

The professor problem would not have been solved by carrying on with the same or revised workshops. Notice how even this limited data gathering from ten professors provides a much clearer picture of what ought to happen, and it makes a case for using the more taxing cross-functional approach. With data, it is easier to "sell" the administration on bringing more players to the table and moving equipment, money, and resources. Note also that the performance analysis effort begins to define subsequent training, providing guidance for a lengthier training needs assessment as the multimedia professional develops subsequent workshops for the faculty.

Another example is provided by Jim Harwood and Steve Bush from IBM. Their challenge was to improve IBM sales professionals' reliance on specified customer relationship processes and methodologies. After they determined exactly what sales people were and were not doing, they asked hard questions. What was getting in the way? This defined their solution system. Table 3.7 presents selected gaps, drivers, and solutions provided by the analysts. One interesting aspect of what Harwood and Bush did was that they systematically sought drivers and causes of the gaps and then gathered a group to help them devise solutions appropriate for those barriers.

◆ ◆ ◆

A visual is a good way to reprise this chapter. Table 3.8 summarizes the points we discussed in this chapter and takes us back to the distinctions between performance analysis and needs assessment drawn in Chapter Two.

TABLE 3.7. IBM SALES SOLUTION SYSTEM DEFINED BY DRIVERS.

Sales Processes	Drivers	Solutions
Identify an opportunity	Don't know how Don't need to do it—not the job they think they're supposed to do	Provide training, job aids, playbook, on-line and print help system Create and distribute executive communication Hold in-person kickoff meetings Distribute newsletter Develop managers
Enter and edit an opportunity	Don't know how Don't need to do it—not the job they think they're supposed to do	Provide training, job aids, playbook, on-line and print help system Conduct a process walk-through Distribute newsletter Develop managers
Enter all opportunities of a certain size in automated tool	Don't know how Don't have authorization	Provide training, job aids, playbook, on-line and print help system Revise requirements and authorizations Communicate changes
Use national standards tables, definitions, and trigger field	Not yet required by tool Don't know it is expected	Communicate need for changes in the tool Update tool Issue executive communications Distribute newsletter

TABLE 3.8. SUMMARY FOR CHAPTER THREE.

	Performance Analysis	*Training Needs Assessment*
Sources	Sponsor, work products, supervisors, customers, job incumbents	Sponsor, model performers, the published literature, documentation, subject matter experts
Kinds of information	Optimals and actuals (basis of directions for the effort), drivers (which enable the definition of solutions)	Optimals, current skills and knowledge (emphasis on optimals to be addressed through education, information, and coaching solutions)
Typical questions	What are you trying to accomplish? What are the important problems? Why isn't it happening? What might get in the way? Do they know how? Do they care?	How do you do it? How might you think about it? What must they know by heart? What can be provided through job aids or documentation?
Outcomes	A description of what it will take to realize the opportunity or solve the problem; a plan that involves individual growth and organizational change. Both are handed off to HR siblings.	The detailed specifications for the education, training, information, or whatever it will take to improve individual's capacity

CHAPTER FOUR

OPPORTUNITIES FOR PERFORMANCE ANALYSIS

VP of sales: We're rolling out a brand new system. I want all our sales people up to speed ASAP, no matter what country they're in. When can we get a course scheduled?

Director of HR: Unsatisfactory is the only way I would describe the way they handle the appraisals. We've trained them. We've exhorted them. Heck, we even redesigned the forms. I don't know what-all to do about it . . .

CEO: Everything is changing here, and we need a management cadre that is ready to thrive in the future. What I want is a plan for professional development for twenty-first-century mid-level managers.

VP of operations: I'm eager to have our people go through a process that will establish some common understandings about directions. In fact, I'm going to put some kind of planning initiative in place. I'll want your help on that.

Focusing on Opportunities

The nature of the request for assistance influences the nature of the performance analysis. Different requirements tilt us toward different approaches and emphases during performance analysis. These requirements aren't radically different, and of course they still revolve around the quest for information about how it ought to be, how it is, and what to do to make it happen. But doesn't it make sense that a study to enable a sales force to sell a new product is different from what you do to contribute to strategic planning or to support the ongoing development of twenty-first-century managers, engineers, or school principals?

This chapter describes four kinds of opportunities and an approach to performance analysis associated with each. Here we'll talk about what the analyst seeks and present some kickoff questions and planning templates matched with each of the four opportunities. The four opportunities are summarized in Table 4.1 with an example of each.

1. *Rollout:* An organization is seeking to introduce something new. It might be a new product, such as software or a computer peripheral or numerical control lathes. Or it might be a new philosophy or perspective on the work, such as a commitment to continuous process improvement or the self-regulation required of mobile employees. The VP of sales at the beginning of the chapter is managing a rollout; other requests might sound like these:

"I want our people to be able to use Lotus Notes. What should we do to make that happen?"

"One of the things that I want to bring to this position is my commitment to global outreach. I want us to move forward on supporting employees as they do short- and longer-term stints worldwide."

"Since the beginning of the year, we've had an influx of families from Somalia. I want to do something for teachers and principals that will help them understand and serve these children and parents."

TABLE 4.1. OPPORTUNITIES AND RATIONALES.

Sample Opportunity	Kind of Opportunity	Rationale
"We're shifting the organization out of a UNIX environment, and there's going to be some significant need for support."	Rollout	The challenge here is to determine swiftly the essence of the change and what it will take to support it.
"I went to a dinner party, and the two women sitting next to me complained about the service they got from us. What's up here? Haven't we done training? What else should we do so I can eat dinner in peace?"	Problem	Something is wrong, and the executive needs to know two things: the general nature of the problem, and the drivers of each aspect of the problem so that a cross-functional program can be launched.
"Our sales are down 11 percent while the industry trend is up 2 percent. We need to do something, and fast."	Problem	The focus here is on finding out why there is a problem, prior to figuring out what to do. What should that "something" be?
"Our hospital administrators must be able to thrive in an environment that is changing radically. How can we prepare them for the new competitive environment?"	People development	The focus here is on the position and on developing the people who hold that position. The challenge is to determine current and future needs and to involve incumbents in the process.
"What I envision is HR helping us with a program to get everybody on the same page here. We need a shared vision, I think."	Strategy development	No specific problem. No new technology or philosophy. No focus on one position or another. This is about broader planning issues.

2. *Problem:* An organization wishes to respond to a performance problem that it has. Perhaps there is a glitch in an ongoing situation, where once things were OK but now are not, perhaps indicated by a dip in sales or an increase in complaints. Or it might be a situation in which mandated training continues but isn't making a dent in the problem. Examples abound: sales drop; accidents increase; scrap production is up; a new leader is dissatisfied with order fulfillment; professors ignore multimedia, even after several workshops on the topic. The HR director at the beginning of the chapter is confronting this dilemma with performance appraisals. He's tried, to no avail. Other requests for assistance might sound like these:

"Do what it takes to get those sales numbers back where
they were."

"I reviewed the order fulfillment numbers and they don't come
close to my goals. What can we do?"

3. *People development:* An organization is focusing attention on a particular position, job, or what the military dubs "billets." Usually, this requirement suggests strategic intention: the leadership is looking ahead, recognizing the critical contributions that people in particular roles bring to continued success. These leaders also note that the world, customers, technology, and products are changing and that they must ensure that their people will be fit to contribute. The CEO in the opening quotes is expressing the need for this type of help. Other requests for assistance might sound like these:

"Our sales people are going to be expected to sell a whole
new line of digital products, and we must help them make their
numbers in this new terrain."

"Insurance companies will not pay for long-term psychodynamic
therapy. We're going to have to find a way to support and develop
our member therapists to cope with these changes."

"The turn of the century is coming. What can we do to be certain
that our managers are ready?"

4. *Strategy development:* Human resources and training professionals find themselves helping the organization or a particular unit to make decisions about direction, values, and alignment. Often this involves facilitating dialogue and process and ensuring that many voices are heard. Although the typical human resources specialist does not typically handle such broad requests, shouldn't we play a part as executives chart this course? The VP of operations at the beginning of the chapter is looking for this kind of contribution. Other requests for assistance might sound like these:

"We're not 100 percent certain about where we stand on this, but
we need some help in establishing options and priorities."

"I think we've been so busy getting it done that we've not stepped back to make certain that we're going in the right direction. We'd like assistance on that process."

"The turn of the century is an important symbol. Surely that marker is an appropriate time to engage in discussion of our mission, vision, and values?"

"I want to make sure that the people closest to the work and in far-flung locations are heard on this issue. They must be part of our plans. I want you to fold them into this process."

How Opportunities Structure Performance Analysis

In Chapter Three we looked at the kinds of information a performance analyst seeks, condensing the inquiry into two large buckets, directions and drivers. Thus far in Chapter Four we've introduced four kinds of typical opportunities. Now let's put them together. The remainder of this chapter provides some templates, shown in Tables 4.2 through 4.5, for handling each type of situation. In each, I focus on the kickoff meeting, assuming that the initial interaction with the sponsor is where we set the effort on a fruitful course. The templates include sample questions for that kickoff session. Tailor these queries to your particular situation and customer, of course.

The first challenge, rollout, is one that dominates business today. Although we most often work on rollouts related to new technology, note that the rollout in Table 4.2 focuses on the introduction of a new way of thinking about and doing the work.

Looking now at Table 4.3, note how different the emphasis is when the professional is charged with solving a problem in an ongoing situation. In the rollout, the sponsor is often excited, worried, eager. When it's a problem, an itch that won't go away, you're more often dealing with the client's impatience. This isn't the first time that the organization has taken a whack at this issue.

The remaining two opportunities, people development and planning, are more strategic. Each involves helping the organization define

TABLE 4.2. ROLLOUT FOCUS.

Opportunity	Rollout
Example	"What I have in mind is something that will help our people understand our new commitment to empowerment. I see your eyebrows raising, and I want you to make sure we have a program that doesn't raise eyebrows, that sincerely helps our folks move in this important direction."
Focus	In a rollout, your emphasis is on figuring out what "it" is that the executive is attempting to bring forward and on anticipating what will *drive success.* You are looking for the beginning outlines of the vision, the *optimals,* of how performance and perspectives will shift if the rollout is successful. Top priority then is to seek the essence of optimals from sources, to compare those views of optimals, and to press leadership toward something resembling the beginnings of consensus on "empowerment" or "teaming" or "conversion to automated records management." The next priority during performance analysis for a rollout is to identify *drivers,* to *anticipate* what might get in the way. What obstacles will appear? What should be put in place to drive toward success?
To the executive:	How do you define empowerment?
	If we had empowered employees, what would they be doing?
	If we were in conversation, now, with an empowered employee, how might he or she be different?
	Do we have employees who are already that way? If so, what do you see them doing? May I work with them?
	Have we captured examples of their thoughts and actions? Is there a way we can begin to create a database of examples?
	What can I read to help me understand empowerment? What has influenced you?
	As we look a little further along, what might get in the way of our move in this direction?
	What will it take to successfully move your people this way?
	Do you think your employees will embrace this shift? Why?
	Where might there be resistance? Why?

TABLE 4.3. PROBLEM FOCUS.

Opportunity	Problem
Example	"My patience with the performance appraisals is gone. Last year we redesigned the form. Two years ago we trained all the managers and supervisors. I'm at my wit's end now. Look at these. They're perfunctory. What are you going to do?"
Focus	When addressing a problem, you must do two things. First, it is critical to nail the problem. Where is it? Where isn't it? In this case, what you're attempting to discern is what's wrong and what's right with the appraisals. That involves comparing optimals with what is currently happening, looking at where we are versus where we want to be. Focus on key problem areas—in this case, the lines in the appraisals that are unsatisfactory. Second, you must answer the question, Why do we have these problems? What are the causes, forces, and drivers associated with each aspect of the problem? Answering this second question allows you to determine who needs to come to the table to solve the problem.
To the executive:	Why are you unhappy with the appraisals?
	What are the biggest problems with the appraisals?
	Where is there a clear statement of what constitutes a "proper" appraisal? What policy documents should we examine?
	Why do you want to tackle this issue now?
	Why do you think that past fixes haven't worked?
	If a supervisor wants to do a bang-up job, to what references and materials can she turn?
	Let's look at the primary problems you've mentioned. What will it take to fix each of them?
	What are the managers' perspectives on appraisals?
	What would job incumbents say we should do to improve the appraisals?
	If you could wave a magic wand over each problem, what would you do?

where it's going, using broader strokes. Table 4.4 illustrates people development; here the emphasis is on nurturing a particular group of employees more than on any predetermined topic or direction.

Human resources and training professionals must help the organization to plan for its future. They do this with a performance analysis that contributes to strategic planning and development. Table 4.5 presents one way of commencing such an effort.

Gearing Performance Analysis to the Opportunity

What follows are templates linked to the four kinds of opportunities. The templates provide suggestions for sources and the order in which you might tap them. They encourage a way of thinking about this early analysis but are certainly not the only way to do it. Customize your approaches with individuals and circumstances in mind. Consider the power of sampling, because many organizations have people and enterprises across the globe.

Stages in PA for a Rollout

Although a performance analysis for a rollout will focus primarily on optimals, its purpose is not to specify exactly what's involved, for example, in operating the system or in doing the work of a teller in an empowered way. Rather, the performance analysis is meant to determine what IBM'ers would call the "5-ups" or key components of the domain. Detailed optimals should be gathered later, during training needs assessment, after the handoff, when those aspects that demand training and information support have been determined.

After you have scoped the general thrust of optimals, move on to find out what it will take to successfully shift the organization and its people in the selected directions. Table 4.6 describes suggested stages for a performance analysis appropriate to the rollout of a new system, technology, or philosophy.

TABLE 4.4. PEOPLE DEVELOPMENT FOCUS.

Opportunity	*People Development*
Example	"I attended a technical training vendor conference last week, and 100 percent of the attendees are shifting some portion of their training to multimedia and distributed formats. Obviously, we will be going in that direction too. But what to do about our 190 instructors and 85 product development people?"
Focus	To facilitate professional development, you must assist the organization in getting a fix on the many directions that might be appropriate for this group of people. Then you must set priorities. There are many ways to conceive the role of the trainer (in this case), or the systems analyst, mental health professional, principal, or hospital administrator. Performance analysis here resembles a rollout, with an emphasis on optimals, but it is targeted at a broader and more strategic level. The effort will be dominated by casting an expansive net for rich optimals and creating a process to involve colleagues in selecting directions and priorities. Given the emphasis on speed, use PA to identify appropriate sources, scope the boundaries of the domain, and begin to envision an approach based on drivers.
To the executive	What do you envision this group of people doing over the next five years? What will they do more of? Less of?
	What challenges do you imagine they will confront?
	How do you expect them to prioritize their work? What accomplishments should be most important to them?
	What shall I read to help me understand your vision?
	What professional associations and experts shall I consult?
	What changes in technology do you view as most significant?
	What changes in relationships do you see with customers? With colleagues across the organization? In the work site?
	How are you collecting examples of desirable practice and thought leadership? How are you making that knowledge available to many?
	Do we have employees who are already approximating good performances? If so, what do you see them doing?
	As you talk about electronic learning, I can't help but wonder how your people will respond. Do you have a sense of their eagerness to move in this direction?
	I anticipate a wide range of definitions for the professional of the future. Who in your organization should be involved in this defining process?

TABLE 4.5. STRATEGY DEVELOPMENT FOCUS.

Opportunity	Strategy Development
Example	"I'm eager to have our people go through a process that will establish a common understanding about directions. I need your help to engage our people with this planning process."
Focus	Strategic planning is about a quest for optimals. The focus during strategic planning is threefold. First, you must lead a process that collects, converges, and articulates perspectives on where the organization or unit is going. Second, that process must have a link to reality and to possibilities and dreams that participants might some day see enacted. It shouldn't be mundane, but it can't entirely be off-the-wall; that means you must engage in some discussion of drivers. Third, you must create and nurture a process that helps many to feel involved.
To the executive	Why do you want to engage your organization in a planning process? How do you want to be involved in this?
	What are your priorities in the future?
	Whose opinions do you want sought during this process?
	What published literature or live sources from the outside do you want to involve in this effort?
	How do you want to be informed about the results as we move along?
	What challenges do you feel are most critical for the industry in general and for your organization in particular?
	What competitive advantages and core competencies do you wish to emphasize? To nurture?
	Are there any benchmarking organizations we should examine?
	To what listservs or on-line communities do you refer? Are there any that are particularly appropriate as we move forward?
	I anticipate a wide range of opinions. How do you want to inform your colleagues about these options? How do you want to move to establishing priorities?
	Your comments tend to center on a few critical trends in development. What do you see as likely to be essential to moving your people in those directions?
	Are you committed to the changes and support it will take?
	Do you think others in the organization share your eagerness regarding these directions?

TABLE 4.6. STAGES FOR ROLLOUT.

Stage	Sources	Some Suggested Questions
One	Customer, sponsor	Why? What will this do for the organization? Why have you decided to go in this direction? What are the essential elements of the shift? Are employees eager for the change? (See Table 4.2 for more suggestions.)
Two	Internal expert	What about this change is most promising? What can it do for the organization? What problems will it solve? What opportunities it will create? How do you want people to use it?
Three	Committee members involved in rollout decisions	What about this change appealed to the committee To you? What is new here? Familiar? What will it do for the employee? The unit? What will it take for a successful rollout? Will your colleagues be enthusiastic about the change?
Four	Vendor, vendor materials and documentation	How does "it" work? How do effective users think about this? What examples do you have of it at work on critical opportunities and issues? When others have begun to use it, what helped make a successful rollout?
Five	The published literature	What does the literature say about this? About the most typical barriers to successful rollout?
Six	Job incumbents and their supervisors	Now that I've described the rollout to you, I'd like your reaction to it. Can you see why the organization is going this way? Do you see benefits for your work? For your unit? What will it help you do? Do you think you have the skills it will take to make the shift?

Stages in PA for a Problem

When you are attempting to solve a problem, the mission is to find out enough about the problem to target questions about drivers. Typically, a client expresses general, all-purpose pain about customer service or performance appraisals; your job then is to swiftly peel the skin off that problem. Where are the problems with customer service? How are the appraisals disappointing? Subsequent questioning about drivers is linked to the particular service complaints or appraisal failures. Table 4.7 describes suggested stages for a performance analysis appropriate to helping customers cure what ails them.

TABLE 4.7. STAGES FOR A PROBLEM.

Stage	Sources	Some Suggested Questions
One	Customer, sponsor	What is the problem? Why are you seeking help now? Why hasn't the problem been solved already? What have you done thus far? (See Figure 4.3 for more questions.)
Two	Records, work products, examined with an expert (if you are not one) or with policies to which the work is compared	What information do we have that defines the problem, that compares what is happening with what ought to be happening? Where are the major problems in these work products? Where are the most costly errors or problems? What would the situation be like, with no problem?
Three	Expert	What would it look like if there were no problem? What should we expect of excellent performance? Why aren't we getting it? Why have past efforts failed? What's in the way?
Four	Job incumbents	What's getting in the way? Why are employees having these problems? If you were king or queen, how would you solve it?
Five	The literature	What does the literature say about the most typical barriers to success in these areas?
Six	Supervisors	I've shared the major problem areas with you. Do they match your perceptions? Why does the organization have each of these problems? What are the causes? What can the organization do? If you ruled the organization, what would you do? Do you care about this problem? Is it one of your priorities?

Examine stage two in the Table 4.7 template. You have a choice for that critical stage. You can define optimals through reviewing policies or by meeting with experts, *or* you can go immediately to an examination of work products or records, something tangible that will help parse the general problem into something more specific. If you can look at the records or products and infer the critical problem areas without formally establishing optimals, then choose that approach. It will save time. This would work for customer service and letters and calls of complaint, for example. In this case, you would likely know enough about expected employee performance to review records and define the problem.

Sometimes, however, you can't just look at the work products and describe key flaws. Perhaps you aren't sufficiently certain about what the standards ought to be. Or you're working in an organization that has a murky picture of what it would like to have happening. Problems with performance appraisals or engineering reports are examples of these more messy and undefined situations. In those cases, stage two should be the swift collection of optimals from policies or models. Then you would make comparisons with work products in stage three.

Stages in PA for People Development

The challenge of performance analysis for people development is to define the future. It is critical to involve as many sources as possible, given your time constraints. If there is little time, the template in Table 4.8 will work for you. If you have more time, add more sources of optimals, including a deeper dig into the literature, and contacts with benchmark organizations.

Stages in PA for Strategy Development

In these situations, as in PA for people development, the focus is on defining the broad strokes of optimals and making certain that the process provides rich information and broad participation. Table 4.9 provides a template for strategy development.

TABLE 4.8. STAGES FOR PEOPLE DEVELOPMENT.

Stage	Sources	Some Suggested Questions
One	Customer, sponsor	Why are you focusing on these employees now? What do you perceive as key skills for the future? What are the emergent challenges they will face? What are they doing now that will endure? In what ways are you collecting best practices? (See Table 4.4 for additional questions.)
Two	The literature, professional associations	What trends are identified? Emergent skills? Perspectives? Emergent challenges? New technologies?
		Where is the disagreement?
Three	Internal and external experts	What trends do you identify? Emergent skills? Perspectives? Emergent challenges? New technologies? From all these, what are the priorities that you associate with this organization and market?
Four	Model performers	What are you doing that strikes people as model? How are you approaching your work? How have you acquired new skills and knowledge? What support did you get from the organization? What do you think will be involved in redefining this role? Have you been asked to collect your perspectives and practices in any ways?
Five	Job incumbents	Do you see the value and benefit in these new roles and competencies? Do you feel ready? What do you think it will take to support your growth in these directions? What might drive or impede your development?

TABLE 4.9. STAGES FOR STRATEGY DEVELOPMENT.

Stage	Sources	Some Suggested Questions
One	Customer, sponsor	Why do you want to engage in strategy development? What do you hope to achieve? How broadly do you want the process to extend? Who are the critical people that must be involved? (See Table 4.5 for additional questions.)
Two	Key managers and leaders	What are the things that distinguish this organization? What are your customers saying about you now? What new things do you want on their lips? What trends will affect your business? Emergent skills? Perspectives? Emergent challenges? New technologies?
Three	Internal and external experts	What will our people be learning about? In what new areas will our people need to develop? Emergent skills? Perspectives? Emergent challenges? New technologies? Emergent opportunities? From all these, what are the priorities?
Four	The literature	Trends? New business opportunities? Emergent skills? Perspectives? Emergent challenges? New technologies? What are benchmark organizations doing to respond?
Five	Supervisors	What worries you? What business opportunities are most interesting? Emergent skills? Perspectives? Emergent challenges? New technologies? Do you feel ready? What do you think it will take to support your growth in these directions? To move the organization in these directions?
Six	Job incumbents	What worries you? What opportunities do you perceive? What emergent skills do you expect to need? New technologies? Do you feel ready? What do you think it will take to support your growth in these directions? To move the organization in these directions?

◆ ◆ ◆

CHAPTER FIVE

PUTTING THE SPEED IN
PERFORMANCE ANALYSIS

Mei: They put this sales skills project in my lap, the one about repeat business and customer focus. It's similar to what they did on customer-oriented selling two years ago. And they've given me precious little time to plan this new effort. I don't want to make a mistake with a program that everybody is scrutinizing.

Floyd: Been there. Of course I believe in study prior to action, but there's no time, none at all. Dagmar e-mailed the specs from Germany for this new operating system and said that we had to have courses ready to go by the end of the quarter. What do I do?

Mei: Prayer comes to mind. Maybe there's a way to do better than sticking our fingers in the wind?

In this chapter, we'll focus on how to plan when there is precious little time for it.

Analysis-Paralysis

A few years ago, when teaching an analysis class at a global high-technology company, I asked each participant to share reasons for taking the class, especially reasons that related to a current project or priority. The sixteenth man introduced himself as an engineer. This got everybody's attention, as this was a company that defined itself though its engineering, and he was the first in the room to identify himself as one. He said something like, "I am responsible for the engineering needs assessment that you may have heard about. It's my job to figure out where we need to go with development for our large and varied engineering population." Everybody turned toward him. This was a very high visibility task.

He continued, "I don't know why, but recently I've felt like I'm losing support for this study. I've been at it for nearly thirteen months now, really working to get it right . . . I guess I'd better find the answer pretty soon."

Really.

Why was he perceiving a loss of interest in his study? He was taking too long. He'd gotten caught up in the study and lost sight of the reasons the organization had asked him to do the study. This engineer had a case of analysis-paralysis, perhaps because he was on a quest for the one "right" answer regarding engineers' needs. What he didn't realize is that there is no single right answer out there for the plucking and that his findings could and should change as conditions in the company, marketplace, and industry evolve. As Marguerite Foxon of Motorola said in a 1997 personal communication, "The more thorough and laborious the needs assessment, the more likely it is to be out of date when completed. These things are works in progress."

The engineer had turned an ongoing responsibility to scan, scope, plan, *and* deliver into an unfulfilled quest for the Holy Grail. While seeking perfection, the engineer for the high-tech company was ignoring a greater priority: to create a system to capture needs and priorities and to report continuously on the implications of what he was learning. In the eyes of those around him, he was disappointing.

Performance analysis could help this engineer. Table 5.1 presents how PA might work for his people development challenge. It is based loosely on Table 4.8, the people development template in Chapter Four. Note that I've changed it for these circumstances, as you would adapt the templates for your situations.

TABLE 5.1. PERFORMANCE ANALYSIS FOR ENGINEERS.

Stage	Sources	Some Suggested Questions
One	Customer, sponsor	Why are you focusing on the development of engineers *now?* What do you hope to accomplish by developing engineers? Are all engineers of equal interest or is one group the focus? What do you see as key skills for the future? What are the emergent challenges? Have you established an on-line community that captures the ideas of thought leaders or enables collaboration between engineers, no matter their location? (See Table 4.4 for additional questions.)
Two	The literature, professional associations	What trends have they identified? Emergent skills? Perspectives? Emergent challenges? New technologies? Additional sources? Implications of worldwide outreach?
Three	Internal and external experts	What trends do you see as most critical? Emergent skills? Perspectives? Emergent challenges? New technologies? From all these, what are the priorities that you associate with this organization and vertical market? Who are the people in this organization who already manifest some of these skills and perspectives? What explicit and tacit know-how is key? Are there any records of this knowledge? How is it maintained? Shared?
Four	Model engineers	You have been identified as possessing skills that are considered "model"; what do you think people are referring to? What strikes them as model about how you do the work? What challenges are emerging? How have you acquired new skills and knowledge? What support did you receive from the organization? What needs to happen to ensure that engineers are contemporary in their skills? What do you think you know and do that distinguished your approaches?
Five	Randomly selected engineers	Here is a description of emerging challenges and competencies. Do you see the value and benefit in these new roles and skills? Do you feel ready? What do you think it will take to support your growth in these directions? What role do you envision for yourself? How might supervisors function differently?

It is critical to report back to the customer throughout the analysis process. For example, you need to brief after the literature review in stage two, engaging the sponsor in a discussion about findings. Then, after stages three and four, write a memo or very short report based on interactions with a handful of internal and external experts and successful engineers. What were their priorities? What resonated for them in the literature? The benefits of frequent reporting, through formal and informal means, are significant, even when the performance analysis is swift. Keep clients and sponsors informed so that they are learning about the mission as you are, increasing the likelihood that you will get support and understanding for subsequent recommendations.

Note that the proposed engineering PA in Table 5.1 didn't yield the details of any training or hiring. Rather, it is likely to generate broad outlines for where resources might be concentrated. A training needs assessment (see Rossett, 1987) would follow to plan instructional and information interventions, with emphasis on what these engineers need to know about telecommunications or object-oriented programming, for example.

Shaving Time Off the Front End

A mantra in corporations and government is "Reduce cycle time." It's the opposite of analysis-paralysis. Whatever it is that is being done, operations managers are pressed to seek ways to shave time off the process. Why should human resources professionals be any different? The same concern for speed that is expected in manufacturing and order fulfillment, for example, is reasonable to demand of training and development too. This chapter presents eight strategies for speeding up the planning process.

1. Clarify the Effort

The number one strategy for saving time is knowing what you're doing. This idea certainly harkens back to time-tested wisdom from Robert Mager. Instead of wandering aimlessly in the land of analysis, gather defined kinds of information from sources like those included in the templates provided in Chapter Four. The nature of the requirements tilts us toward particular patterns of effort and levels of specificity in our questions. Note, for example, that even though the pattern of sources and stages in Table 5.1 and Table 5.2 (which we will see later) are similar, the specificity is different. Each approach is influenced by the nature of the initial request and by how much is known at the get-go.

The conceptual framework in Chapter Three and the templates in Chapter Four provide guidance. Although you shouldn't follow the templates religiously, they do suggest a path that you can modify, as I did with the engineering initiative detailed in Table 5.1.

Let's look in on Floyd and Mei as they continue to discuss Floyd's project, the rollout of a new operating system across a large, global organization.

Floyd: I've got to do some kind of analysis before I roll out the operating system. I decided to do a survey. I'll use e-mail; that way I can reach everybody fast. They're pushing me hard.

Mei: Yeah, it's a good idea to get something out there, like a survey. People want us to seek their input. And using e-mail is a good idea. Have you sent it out yet?

Floyd: Well, I don't know what questions to put on the survey. And I wonder if they'll respond, since I'll know who the e-mail is coming from. Using e-mail felt right-on to begin with, but now I'm not so sure. Maybe it would be better to run some groups? Whatever I do, it's got to be fast.

What's Floyd's problem? Floyd doesn't know what he's looking for. He wants to do a study, but it appears to be a study for the study's sake, with little clarity about the substantive purposes. What information is he trying to gather? What questions is he trying to answer? What sources are critical? Beyond showing "people" that he "cares" about their opinions, and exerting effort during his hours at work, what is he likely to accomplish with an unfocused inquiry? Not much. And he produces cynicism in an organization that perceives no connection between his inquiry and the resulting programs.

How could Floyd sharpen his approach? Table 5.2 presents one of many possibilities.

Because it is a rollout, Floyd should focus attention on a preliminary definition of "it," in this case, of the new operating system. Simultaneously, he must scan for performance drivers and potential obstacles. He can gather both kinds of information from the same sources, at the same time—a sure time-saver.

Floyd deviates from the rollout template in Table 4.6 in two ways. First, after meeting with the sponsor, he decides to review the minutes of the meeting of the internal committee charged with the leap to the new operating system. He will save time by not meeting individually with committee members; he's hoping that the minutes captured the issues about which he is most concerned—why they are switching to the new system, and priority uses. If the minutes are sketchy or unclear, Floyd can contact members for further explanations.

The other departure from the template is that Floyd skips the review of related literature. He's depending on the vendor for information about operating system rollouts, both those specific to their system and lessons from the operating system domain in general. If that's not forthcoming, then a quick trip to the literature will enhance planning.

The new and improved Floyd (in Table 5.2) knows what he's after and uses focused questions that reflect this clarity. He picks his techniques for gathering information based on what he's looking for. And he's on target to complete the performance analysis speedily. Even assuming the usual bumps and glitches, Floyd could complete the planning shown in Table 5.2 in a few business days.

Let's think about Mei's comment, "People want us to seek their input." They do, but not just so that they can experience the thrill of being asked. Most want their input to contribute to tangible recommendations, options, and suggestions. Making a show of interest doesn't substitute for authentic uses of the data. In fact, conducting numerous surveys without distributing meaningful results to the respondents will eventually produce more cynicism than appreciation. That's how organizations find themselves suffering from "survey satiation."

TABLE 5.2. FLOYD'S OPERATING SYSTEM ROLLOUT.

Stage	Sources	Some Suggested Questions
One	Customer, sponsor	What is unique about this operating system (OS)? Why have you decided to go in this direction? What are the essential elements and benefits associated with the shift? What do you want different employee groups to do with the system? What do you think must be done to make this a successful rollout here and globally? (See Table 4.2 for more questions.)
Two	Review of minutes associated with the OS decision	Examine minutes related to the decision to go with the new OS, the new technical specifications, how the new differs from the current OS, expectations for vendor performance, and any concerns associated with rollout. Seek why they've picked it, identify key elements, concerns, vendor promises.
Three	Internal expert or executive closest to the technical details associated with the new OS	What about this change is most promising? What can it do for the organization? What problems will it solve? How do you want people to use it? What are some of the costs and benefits? What is the anticipated impact on processes? As we think about introducing people to the OS, what will it take to increase their comfort and use?
Four	Vendor, vendor materials and documentation	This is Floyd's opportunity to capture details associated with the OS and to focus on lessons learned from rollouts in other organizations. How does it enable _____? How does it work? When others have begun to use it, what helped make a successful rollout?
Five	Job incumbents— focus groups with employees randomly pulled from the organization	Now that I've described the new OS, I'd like your reaction to it. Can you see why the organization has made the switch? Do you see benefits? Do you think you have the skills it will take to make the shift? What questions and concerns do you have? What support would help you move in this direction?

2. Repurpose Existing Data

Years ago, I got a phone call from a human resources manager charged with developing a safety program for five manufacturing plants. Let's call her Emma. Moved by the importance of the effort, Emma had been studying the situation for months and had commandeered a room for the assembled materials and reports associated with safety in manufacturing. Her treasure trove was overwhelming. She was awash in statements about the directions a safety program might take, including optimals, best practices, and actuals, detailing where efforts have gone wrong.

What Emma lacked was how these optimals related to *her* company. Where were the different plants messing up? Where were employees doing well and not so well? Where and when were the accidents and near-misses? What were the gaps in performance associated with the employees in and across plants? What might be causing the documented unsafe moments and actions? The detailed optimals would eventually prove useful, but later, in training needs assessment, after Emma's having established the nature of the problems and their drivers. Then she could pluck the appropriate optimals from her room.

How should Emma proceed with her charge to improve safety in her organization? Table 5.3 details recommendations for Emma. The suggestions are based on Table 4.7, the performance problem template in Chapter Four.

Although Table 4.7 was the jumping-off point for these recommendations, note that this PA is tailored to Emma's situation. For example, I suggest that she rely heavily on existing information. This will enable her to customize her study to her plants and their circumstances. In the early stages of the analysis, Emma must swiftly find out where safety is an issue and where it isn't. She does this by querying the sponsor and reviewing insurance claims and regulatory and accident reports. They tell her where the problems, accidents, and weaknesses are. It is these extant documents that make her efforts meaningful to the organization and enable her to save time. There are many kinds of data that you can repurpose in this way: accident reports like those Emma

Putting the Speed in Performance Analysis

TABLE 5.3. EMMA'S SAFETY CHALLENGE.

Stage	Sources	Some Suggested Questions
One	Customer, sponsor	Why do you want to focus on safety now? Why hasn't the problem been solved already? I looked at our current safety program and wonder what your thoughts are about it. What are our strengths and weaknesses in this area now? Where can we find the details about current safe and unsafe situations and actions? (See Table 4.3 for more questions.)
Two	Regulatory reports	Review the documents for answers to the following: What are we doing right? Wrong? What did outside evaluators pinpoint? What did they recommend? Where are the most grievous errors or problems?
Three	Accident reports, insurance claims, employee complaints	Review the documents for answers to the following: What are our problems? Where are employees getting hurt? What are the patterns? What situations and actions are unsafe?
Four	Job incumbents	What is causing the major problems [identified in stages one through three]? Why are employees having these problems? If you were king or queen, how would you solve each of them?
Five	The literature	What does the literature say about the most typical barriers to success in these areas? What are the recommendations?
Six	Supervisors	I've shared the major problem areas with you, based on my review of reports and claims. Do they match your perceptions? Why does the organization have each of these problems? What are the causes? What can the organization do? If you ruled the organization, what would you do? How might the organization make safety a higher priority? Is it one of your priorities?

reviewed, exit interviews with employees, insurance claims, and letters and e-mails from customers.

There is little need for Emma to spend time studying optimals at this point. She's already done that, to little avail, and safe optimals, at the level of detail she needs *in a PA,* are pretty obvious: no burns; retain digits on fingers; job aids attached to dangerous equipment; and so on. Capturing the details of safe operations associated with particular tasks or machinery should happen during the training needs assessment.

Stage five in Table 5.3 is interesting. I recommend that Emma take some time to look into the literature on the causes associated with the manufacturing safety issues she unearths in the previous stages. What does the literature say about critical success factors for manufacturing safety? Although she'd done some prior examination of the literature, what she found wasn't what she needed. In a performance analysis, she wants to know about recurring barriers and drivers for these kinds of safety challenges. That's where her attention is directed in stage five.

The real challenges in Emma's performance analysis are twofold: first, to swiftly find the major safety snafus, and second, to determine why they exist. The first aspect doesn't have to be that time-consuming: use existing accident data. The second critical part of the PA depends on getting answers to questions from several sources close to the work and danger—in this case, job incumbents, supervisors, and the literature. Once she knows why things go wrong, Emma will be able to figure out what the organization must do. She might contract for training and job aids in some areas, new equipment and gear in others, and supervisory development, enhanced recognition programs, and reengineered processes for still others.

3. Use "Straw," Not Tabula Rasa

The following dialogue is typical:

Mei: Thanks so much for being willing to talk to me about sales strategies for ensuring repeat business. You're pretty famous in the company for doing that, so I wanted to be sure to talk to you.

Rick: No problem, Mei. What can I do for you?

Mei: Two things, really. I want to know how you do it, and I want to know why you think so many of our sales staff have problems in this area. Let's start with what you do to ensure repeat business.

Rick: Never really thought about it much. Just seems a good thing to do, somehow easier to keep adding onto what you already have. I'm a little shy, so I prefer talking to people I know more than people I don't. Uh, sorry. Not sure, really.

Mei: What do you do that is different in the way you service accounts, perhaps?

Rick: Don't know that I do anything special . . .

Mei: Why don't you describe what you typically do for the customers who are most likely to become repeat customers?

Rick: Just the usual. Lots of calls, of course, to make sure things are going OK. I just try to be me, and it seems to work pretty good.

Mei is having a devil of time drawing anything useful and tangible from Rick. When she eventually despairs of acquiring direction about optimals from him and switches to a question about why so many sales people fail to create repeat business, he likely will continue to be taciturn. The fact is that many sources, whether incumbents, sponsors, or experts, are less than eloquent about what it is they know and do. You can lose a lot of time here, a real problem when speed counts.

An effective strategy is to use "straw": give your sources something to which to respond. It might be an outline, a video interaction, a diagram, technical specifications, or a set of symptoms and recommended tests. What's important is that it provides sufficient detail to stimulate the source to respond. What often results is a surprising flood of corrections, amendments, agreement and disagreement. For example, a description of how one salesperson might approach securing repeated business is likely to stimulate Rick to describe how he does it, with specifics on what's similar to and different from the "straw."

Several professionals at Boeing, for example, described how they used video to elicit responses from experts, managers, and job incumbents. For a manufacturing challenge, they taped processes and asked their "talent" to talk about what they were doing and why. This generated useful comments and organizational support for the effort. It made the domain and challenge more tangible.

4. Establish Hypotheses and Test Them with Sources

Jim Harwood of IBM calls it fastpathing. I call it rearview validation. Either way, it's a slick way of saving time. Harwood and Ann Leon, both of IBM, were charged with the global rollout for an automated skills tool. They had a considerable change-management challenge on their hands and no time. What they did was to generate a massive amount of "straw," based on their experiences and brief and pointed discussions with the experts who had used the tool in Australia and in other pilots. Harwood and Leon guessed gaps, guestimated drivers and barriers, and then were so bold as to generate a solution system based on these hypotheses. They produced a report that was so much "straw" that it was flammable.

Here is where it gets interesting. They then gathered a group of irreverent and knowledgeable people from across the organization and charged these people with checking out Harwood and Leon's assumptions. With what did they agree and disagree? What had they forgotten? Did they see it the way that Harwood and Leon saw it? How realistic were the approaches they proposed and the drivers on which those approaches were predicated? What additional data should be collected? Basically, Harwood and Leon had gathered people to rewrite the report, to craft a better story about what needed to be done to support the rollout of the software, to inform them as to how much more data needed to be collected. Harwood reports that their hypotheses were mostly on point, that they saved time, and that this planning approach resulted in a sound rollout.

5. Establish a System for Virtual Analyses

Maybe the analysis process is too customer driven. I know that those words are heresy, and perhaps they are a bit extreme, but there's an important theme here, relating to the role of the human resources professional. Should we *wait* for requests from customers for the services that we provide? Should we perceive ourselves as dependent on customer initiatives for the genesis of performance improvement programs? Should our first reckoning of a new program take place when we are requested to support it in some way?

I don't think so. Although there will always be a significant number of programs that are born because an executive wants them, wouldn't the organization and its people be better off if those kinds of programs represented a dwindling percentage, if training and human resources development professionals were playing a more strategic role? Rather than wait, shouldn't we anticipate?

How do we do that? We do it through *continuous* formal and informal collection of data from key sources. We ask questions like these: What do sources see as emergent trends, changes, new skill and knowledge areas, competitive arenas, emerging technology? Where are our current problems and successes? What is working? What isn't? What's getting in the way? How are employees perceiving the current systems and the changes that lurk in the wings? Virtual analysis collects this information in the normal course of doing business, saving time because the data are already on hand when a need appears or a request for assistance is presented.

A program for a military contractor provides an example. The human resources department is always involved in collecting information about new directions, current performance, and obstacles and drivers. They do this in post-class evaluations, regularly scheduled focus groups with employees, regularly scheduled interviews with executives, and on-line surveys. These data are at the ready, no matter what comes up, such as a question about professional development priorities for engineers, or about readiness for the plunge into digital and away from analog, or about shifting expectations to rely upon team performance. The human resources professionals save time because they already know so much. *Their performance analysis process is more one of confirming and extending than of generating anew.*

So the press here is to establish a system to ensure ongoing collection of data. Do you regularly meet with leaders in the organization?

Do you scan the literature associated with the business your organization is in? Do you read the annual report? Do you add items to corporate surveys and pore over survey results for their implications for performance improvement? Do you ask pointed questions about drivers when you find yourself at a luncheon table with associates? Do you have a system to capture these data and feed them back for additional reactions? Do you know who else in the organization is asking related questions and how to access their data, should you need it? Have you established a system to repurpose the virtual data? Chapter Seven focuses on the implications of technology for virtual performance analysis.

6. Generalize

Another time-saving technique is to use a cookie cutter—that is, to assume that what you discover through systematic study in one area has implications and richness for others. This information becomes the "straw" for presentation to other regions and groups of employees. Although you may be making quite a leap when you generalize this way, more often than not there are similarities in responses to a new operating system, for example, or in the causes of unsafe conditions in manufacturing plants. The important point is to use one source to frame up possibilities and then to validate the generalizations with other sources.

Some colleagues at a computer company used this approach to plan skills development for their global sales organization. Initially, they focused their analysis energy in one part of the United States. When their findings from this region were presented to others across North America and even worldwide, the typical response was accord. More of the findings fit than not. And when the fit was off, sales people filled in descriptions more relevant to their terrain.

7. Collapse the Steps

Early in this book I emphasized the importance of systematic processes, in which data are gathered and the output of one phase serves as input for the next. This method is deliberate, desirable, and appropriate. But it is not always feasible.

One way to speed up the process is to bring key players together to answer critical questions right at the beginning. Peter Senge, in the handbook that supports his *Fifth Discipline*, encourages just this kind of process. Put a potential solution system on the table and then do the kinds of hard querying that make certain the solution is pointed in the right directions and predicated on the true drivers. If we were talking about a rollout about our assumptions about drivers, we might ask

Is this an apt description of the situation?

What problems might stump the employees?

If we ruled the universe around here, what are all the things we should do to ensure that this successfully contributes to performance?

What is likely to contribute to employees' ability to handle this change?

One year from now, what will we wish they knew and did?

One year from now, what could have gotten in the way of their effective movement in this direction?

Now, as we look at the solution that is proposed, ask the following questions:

Will this system successfully introduce the change?

Does it touch all the bases?

Will the programs we're proposing result in a successful rollout?

Do our plans match your understanding of what works in this culture?

8. Rely on Automation to Speed the Process

Mark Fulop, Kelly Loop-Bartick, and I published an article about automated analysis in *Performance Improvement* (July 1997). We told the story of constructing a site on the World Wide Web to do an analysis with university health educators across North America. In a nutshell, questions and responses were posted at a Web site in order to encourage broad participation and comment. As new responses were generated, they too were posted. A gatekeeper monitored the process, making certain that things flowed smoothly and that comments furthered the goals of the effort and were clear. Once diverse and rich information had been collected, the team turned to expert health educators with experience on the Web. They helped to focus and tame the abundant possibilities. The resulting Web site surprised its developers, as it placed more emphasis on facilitating dialogue and research between institutions through chats and newsgroups and less on providing static health information. What's important is that it worked and that many miles were leapfrogged and many people were involved in speedy fashion.

Automation is a very good way to save time. An example is the performance support tool associated with this book and available at the Jossey-Bass Web site. Its purpose is to help you do some of the things you've been reading about. I've done many front-end studies, but I still turn to an automated tool because it saves me time. It also encourages me to remember sources and queries that I might skip in haste. Chapter Seven discusses the topic of automated data collection, communications, and analysis.

Professional Hesitations About Quick-and-Dirty Analyses

The demands on a human resources and training professional can be contradictory; for example, to study prior to action and to provide speedy service to customers in need. The remainder of this chapter is a response to concerns you might be having.

I Can't Be Certain

No, you can't. But when would you be 100 percent certain? It is the rare analytical technique—at least among those involving people in organizations, not laboratories—that results in absolute certainty, and even then, the certainty doesn't last very long. What you're seeking is to gather more information than you had when you began, to transcend habit and bias, to involve a wide array of sources, and to create a textured picture of the possibilities. You're taking a grainy picture that strengthens your recommendations and provides ammunition for the cross-functional efforts that lie ahead.

I Didn't Talk to Everybody

You *shouldn't* talk to everybody, not if you have any hopes of timely performance. Instead, use sampling; that is, randomly pull representatives of the larger population you're concerned about. Then you are able to generalize from their responses to the larger group that they represent. The power is in randomization, because every person in the group has an equally good chance of being selected to provide their view of the situation.

Using sampling doesn't mean that you can't talk to a reflective person here, a renegade there, or an expert over there. They provide other kinds of perspectives. But if you wish to get a broader view of how the lathe operators or bank tellers or frontline supervisors or teachers see it, you will need to pull randomly from the larger population. Stop gathering data when the information begins to be repetitious.

How Will I Sell to a Skeptical Sponsor?

Most sponsors prefer speed to just about anything. Occasionally you'll come across a sponsor who demands large numbers. In that case, give them to him or her. This provides an opportunity to use a well-designed e-mail survey (see Chapter Seven). Usually, however, if you can point to the involvement of several worthy sources in interviews and focus groups, to randomization, triangulation, and, most important, answers to obviously useful questions, the sponsor will appreciate what you're doing.

Interpretation is always tricky. An article in the *New Yorker* (Hertzberg, 1998) makes this point. The editors commissioned a broad opinion survey of the American public that they called "a fearless inquiry into whatever" (p. 27). Let's take their question "Do you believe in God?" Of the respondents in the group they dubbed Main Street, 92 percent answered in the affirmative; 61 percent of *New Yorker* readers, a well-educated group the editors called High Street, said they believe in God. The magazine then provides examples of the art of interpretation. One writer could take those numbers and note that High Street, a group many would describe as elitist and unlike Middle America, is really God fearing. Note the strong majority (61 percent) affirming their belief in God. Another writer could use the same numbers to point out the striking difference (92 percent versus 61 percent) between educated and middle America.

Which is it? There's no right answer here, as is the case with so much of the work that we do. What's important is that you solicit and present opinions. It's up to you and the customer to discuss alternative interpretations.

Isn't There More I Could Do?

There's always more that could be done. Remember that this is the initial scoping of the effort, during which you set direction for the effort and determine who ought to be involved. As I've said before, the task during performance analysis is to determine, from the perspective of judiciously selected sources, what people ought to be doing and considering. Having done so, you can then marshal, direct, and even save resources for the subsequent training needs assessment and collaboration across units that follow.

◆ ◆ ◆

You *can* shave time off the front end. Here's how you do it:

Get clear about where you're going. What kinds of information are you seeking? In what ways is this source likely to be most helpful? How can you enhance the political benefits of the interactions? Time is wasted in aimless meandering.

Repurpose existing data that reside in the organization. Look to exit interviews, sales records, customer feedback, work products. There is much there that gives you a quick picture of the current situation, often from several sources. It's always quicker and cheaper to repurpose existing data than to gather anew.

Capitalize on what you and other wise people know by putting "straw" out there for reactions and improvement. Most sources need assistance in being helpful to you. Provide outlines, hypotheses, schematics, suggested ways of handling challenges—your sources will have much to say about what you've proposed.

Engage in virtual performance analyses. Continuously gather trends, directions, problems, issues, and causes so that you are never surprised when a request for assistance appears.

Use automation to reach out, to gather and analyze data.

Gather examples of successful analyses and use them to spread the benefits of this kind of thoughtful approach.

CHAPTER SIX

COMMUNICATING TO GATHER INFORMATION AND SUPPORT

Axel: Remember I told you I was going out to the plants in Mexico and Ontario to interview foremen and engineers? All part of the front end for the safety project. Well, it went really well— much to my surprise.

Ludmila: I remember that you were worried. I think you said you were thinking about not going, or using an e-mail survey or something. These things can be nasty when they go south.

Axel: That's why I was worried. Once I had a focus group that ran amok—I had a near mutiny on my hands. And a couple of times I've had experts who refused to tell me much of anything at all. Now this didn't happen to me, but I heard about a human resources guy who had a survey that bounced back from the field because he used the wrong terminology. There's more to this than just scheduling some meetings or shipping out some surveys.

In this chapter, we focus on the communications that underpin analysis. We'll start with a quick tour of the methods used to gather information: interviews and focus groups, observations, surveys, and examination of existing data and work products. Then we'll focus on general communications principles that cut across these methods, highlighting the perspectives of different sources.

Methods for Gathering Information and Support

There are four methods for gathering information and support during analysis. What I'll do here is briefly describe them and then make some comparisons, focusing particularly on their proclivities for speediness and usefulness during PA. More detailed treatment of these methods is provided in my book *Training Needs Assessment*.

Interviews and Focus Groups

Interviews are the most common way of gathering performance analysis data; focus groups, though popular, are less typical. Table 6.1 is a brief comparison of interviews and focus groups.

During an interview, one individual asks questions of another in order to seek opinions. Not surprisingly, we tend to be interested in those factors that are not observable or obvious, such as expertise, feelings and opinions, and data often labeled as qualitative or tacit. Often we're interviewing or running a group to make manifest the skills, perspectives, performance drivers, and cultural forces of which respondents aren't consciously aware. For example, we might ask an executive if her regional managers are confident about their abilities to manage now that the organization is using technology to distribute information more broadly. Or you might use an interview to ask individual doctors if they share executives' enthusiasm regarding the shift to hospital care teams headed by nurses. Or you might use interviews or focus groups to seek examples of the strategies that contract negotiators use to successfully hold the line on costs.

Focus groups provide an opportunity to gather a group representing, for example, different perspectives, geographic regions, or organizational

TABLE 6.1. INTERVIEWS AND FOCUS GROUPS.

	Interviews	*Focus Groups*
Kinds of information	Defines direction (optimals and actuals) and drivers. Very useful for establishing relationships and defining subsequent ways of working together.	Typically used for defining optimals and for gaining consensus across organizations and geographic areas.
Benefits	Shows commitment to opinions beyond your own or the executive's. Enables probing for the meaning behind statements.	More efficient way to involve many individuals and organizations in planning.
Limitations	Costly in time and resources. Some respondents are hesitant to share opinions; they sometimes fear what you'll do with their views. There's no anonymity in an interview, of course. If your project isn't their priority, some sources are reluctant.	Gathering disparate people and viewpoints can lead to chaos and to the hardening of positions instead of to consensus. People may not offer honest opinions. Not everybody is adept at leading focus groups. Anonymity is nonexistent, and opinions can become public.
PA or TNA?	Used for gathering information during PA and TNA.	Although they are common as general kickoff sessions for both PA and TNA, focus groups are more often used in TNA, as they are appropriate for simultaneously gathering detailed information about skills and knowledge and encouraging buy-in.
Chronology	Use interviews at the beginning of the analysis, and throughout.	A focus group is not the best way to launch your quest for optimals (though many disagree). Better to commence with interviews with experts and review of documents, and then, after you are familiar with all the likely views, assemble a group.

affiliations. The challenge is to garner diverse wisdom and views without creating or solidifying chasms between constituencies.

The heart of interviews and focus groups is the questions. Interviews and group sessions should be driven by the purposes of the interaction and the desire to establish positive working relationships. Strauss, Schatzman, Bucher, and Sabshin (1981) identify four kinds of questions: hypothetical, devil's advocate, ideal position, and interpretive. To their four, I add two: flawed position questions and straw questions. Table 6.2 presents each type with a sample question for an interview with Mick Reynolds, a senior executive for a large retail superstore. Mick is eager to launch yet another customer service initiative. (We'll meet Vicente Mata, one of his managers, later in this chapter.)

Another key aspect of communicating during interviews and focus groups is the use of probing questions. A probe is a follow-up question. Notice how the analyst uses two probes for drivers with Mick:

Mick: . . . supervisors who understand the active role they must play in customer service. We've got some who do it and others who just don't, or won't, maybe.

Analyst: What appears to be the difference between supervisors who are and those who aren't playing an active customer service role?

Mick: I'm not sure. Maybe they don't know how to do it, or fear that the reps will see it as an intrusion.

Analyst: Have you ever asked the reps how they perceive supervisors who play more active roles during customer service? When reps are trained, what messages are conveyed about roles?

Think about the focus group as the big brother or sister of the interview. Many of the benefits of the methods are the same. Both can be employed to establish rapport and buy-in and to gather information from constituents. As you can see from the interaction with Mick, questions move the effort forward, as the professional drills into topics.

Focus groups can be particularly tricky, however. There's usually one of you and several of them. Managing several people, with several and occasionally parochial perspectives, and keeping track of progress can be daunting.

TABLE 6.2. SIX KINDS OF QUESTIONS
FOR INTERVIEWS AND FOCUS GROUPS.

Type of Question	Analyst Queries
Hypothetical questions ask how the respondent might want the situation handled. Use the words *how might, what if, suppose.*	Suppose that the organization had hit a home run with the customer services program rolled out nearly two years ago. What would you be seeing in the organization now? How might things work differently?
Ideal position questions press the interviewee to describe how he or she wishes it would be.	Picture yourself in one of our stores. Imagine that you are witnessing stellar customer service. What's going on?
Devil's advocate questions press the interviewee to take a position he or she might not have considered or to take the opposite position.	Customer service is like motherhood and apple pie. What if we didn't bother to tackle the issue? How would things be different? What if we did everything but training? What would that look like?
Flawed position questions press the interviewee to speculate on the opposite of the desired state.	Back to the store. But this time it's not a good customer service picture; in fact, it's very bad. You are upset about what you see. What's going on? Detail examples of flawed customer service.
Interpretive questions tie together some of what you've been hearing and ask the respondent for reactions.	Your references to training suggest that you think that employees aren't responding rapidly and well because they don't know how to do so. Is that accurate? Do you think they lack skills in this area? Is that the key factor?
Straw questions give the interviewee something to respond to. It might be a list, a visual, an audio interaction, or the like.	I want you to listen to this audio interaction and give me a sense of whether or not you think the supervisor is doing what's necessary to ensure good customer service. Please tell me what you like and don't like.

Use interviews and review of related documents to set the stage for focus groups. Visit or call key participants prior to the gathering. Determine ahead of time what they know and care about. Seek commonalties and distinctions. Look for hot buttons. When you commence with a group meeting, there is a tendency for individuals to swiftly home in on those areas in which they disagree. You don't want to be surprised. It's far better to be aware and prepared for the inevitable abrasions that arise when varied constituencies are represented.

Observations

There's much to be gained from being vigilant in the field. Two forms of observation are useful. Observing people at work is one type; scrutinizing documents is the other.

Watching people at work will provide information about the nature of the work and what might be driving or impeding effective performance. For example, if you were asked to improve the performance of hotel employees during check-in, observation would be very useful. Table 6.3 presents possible stages for attacking this problem.

When you are in that hotel lobby, you want to take controlled visual snapshots of the situation, focused by what you had learned in the prior stages of the performance analysis. Focus on those areas mentioned by the executive and customers. What do you see? You're seeking the drivers of the situation. There are limited possibilities. Might the employees not know what to do? Might the computer system be foiling them? Might their training or policies lead them to behave in ways that aren't congruent with current customer preferences? For example, are they engaging in friendly, exact explications about hotel amenities when business travelers are longing to be lounging in their rooms?

If you can watch unobserved and without influencing performance, you'll gather important information about drivers. Work patterns and assignments will be obvious. Missing information or clunky computer systems will be obvious too. If you decide to inform sources that you'll be with them, at first you'll witness their attempts at engaging in optimal check-in activities. If they perform in ways that avoid the customer

TABLE 6.3. STAGES IN ANALYSIS FOR HOTEL CHECK-IN.

Stage	Sources	What to Seek
One	Sponsor	Why address check-in now? What's the problem? What is the sponsor hoping to accomplish? Does she have any sense of the driver(s) of the problems?
Two	Customer complaints	Examine documents that reflect the concerns of customers and the sponsor. What are they emphasizing? Around what problems do they cluster?
Three	Observation of desk personnel	Do you see the issues that were noted in customer comments? Can you see trends in drivers of these problems?
Four	Interviews with desk personnel and supervisors	Seek the drivers of the problems identified in customer letters and calls.
Five	Review of training materials	Seek the details of what people are taught about issues related to the identified problems.
Six	Review of policies	What does the organization tell its people is required?

complaint areas when you're there *and* they're exerting special effort, then it's obvious that skill and knowledge aren't the barriers and that training won't solve this problem. Look to the other possibilities, such as supervision, computer software, or a new population of guests with different priorities.

You can use observations of people at work to gather data about current or desired performance, but they are time-consuming and might be best saved for training needs assessment, when you know that you'll be rolling out training or information to support improved performance. For example, if you discovered during analysis that a problem was caused by an absence of knowledge about troubleshooting the computer check-in system, then during training needs assessment you might return to watch effective performers in order to specify the details of optimal effort.

Documents and work products are also the objects of our visual attention. They are a rich and bargain-priced source of information about what's currently going on and what we might want to see. As you can see in Table 6.3, feedback from customers, captured in the record of their comments, is an early and relevant source for targeting the effort to where the pain resides.

Occasionally, you'll be able to infer causes from a pattern in this extant data; for example, if insurance claims are limited to one piece of equipment in a factory, you might begin to infer a cause associated with the equipment.

When you're looking at documents, you are examining the "stuff" of the organization. Examples abound and are limited only by your imagination and access. Let's look at some possibilities for document sources in Table 6.4.

There are many other possible sources, such as exit interviews, performance appraisals, and annual reports. Although nobody would deny

TABLE 6.4. CHALLENGES AND SUGGESTED DOCUMENT SOURCES.

Challenge	Document Sources
The vice president of global training and development for a pharmaceutical company wants to plan strategies to ensure that her employees and those assigned in business units across the world have state-of-the-art capabilities. She's eager to ensure quality and consistency of work.	Review existing training standards. Examine instructor and student course materials. Examine computer records regarding professional development and educational history. Review database of favored approaches. Review vision statement and strategic plan prepared by the VP. Review competencies published by professional associations. Review publications that discuss emergent challenges and competencies.
An executive for an aerospace manufacturing firm is eager to improve safety.	Review accident records. Review insurance claims. Review supervisory reports. Examine reports filed by OSHA. Examine reports written by the company in response to OSHA concerns.
Engineers are not writing satisfactory reports, in the opinion of their leaders. The leadership wants a class to improve the reports. You decide to look into it before scheduling the class.	Review randomly pulled reports. Review reports identified as optimal. Review policies associated with reports. Review on-line templates and boilerplate. Review the feedback related to these concerns.

you access to the annual report, it's not unusual to have roadblocks pop up when you seek to examine appraisals or exit interviews or even reports written by engineers or analysts. Because you don't need to associate the individuals' names with their output, tell the holders of the documents that they can mask the identity of employees prior to providing the reports.

Documents should not be used in isolation from other sources of information. After you have determined patterns in performance or customer reaction or exit interviews, it's critical to talk to those who are involved or implicated. You will likely turn to interviews or focus groups as follow-up.

Surveys

In many organizations, surveys aren't popular with employees. There are two reasons for the low esteem in which they are held. The first is that there are too many surveys. The second is that too little happens as a result of the surveys. If you want results and want to avoid contributing to cynicism in the organization, make certain to survey judiciously and provide some value to participants. Tell them what you found. Describe the shift in program emphases that resulted. Detail a course of action that might not have been taken or that an executive might not have pursued without the data from the surveys.

My focus here is going to be on surveys for performance analysis. As you know, in PA we're concerned about quickly figuring out what to do. Surveys serve that effort in a particular way, enabling us to reach out to large numbers for their priorities and opinions. After we have gathered opinions from leaders, documents, benchmarks, and experts, a survey enables us to place options in front of many of the people doing and supervising the work.

Don't wait until the effort is requested. Anticipate that wise executives will want to know the major development needs within their organizations. Here is the opportunity for virtual analysis, in this case through surveys, as you look for direction regarding development for the engineers or hospital administrators or loan officers or training and

development professionals of the twenty-first century. While seeking priorities, we can also ask respondents to speculate on forces that block or
might impede progress. Let's look at an example.

Table 6.5 represents the stages in a performance analysis associated
with professional growth for training and development professionals in
a global corporation. The task was presented like this: "We want to
move our training and development professionals in some distinct ways.
We're interested in performance, consultation, and technology. What
we don't know is where these professionals are on all this." Table 6.5
presents stages associated with the entire PA effort; the survey (stage six),
comprising the forced-choice options you see in Tables 6.6a and 6.6b,
was based on what was learned early on in the performance analysis.

This partial survey would be distributed anonymously. Note that the
questions in Table 6.6a seek perspectives and priorities. Table 6.6b asks
training professionals to anticipate performance drivers for their transformation.

Effective Communications

Four principles should drive the way we communicate during performance analysis:

1. Know your sources.
2. Be authentic.
3. Remember that performance analysis might be perceived as threat-
   ening, controversial, and intrusive.
4. Emphasize planning; it is at the heart of effective communications.

Know Your Sources

No surprise here, but still a challenge. Before you go out in the field,
consider the following questions:

Who are the sources and what are their perspectives?

Are they delighted to participate? Are they hesitant? Why?

Where are their managers on this topic?

TABLE 6.5. STAGES IN ANALYSIS FOR GLOBAL TRAINING AND DEVELOPMENT PROFESSIONALS.

Stage	Sources	What to Seek
One	Sponsor(s)	Why now? What are they hoping to accomplish? What are the priority directions for their training and development professionals? Any problems they're seeking to solve? Any models or benchmarks? Any literature that is influential?
Two	The literature or an expert or consultant	Examine articles, books, and contributions to professional associations for emergent competencies. What are they emphasizing? Around what topics and concerns do authorities' opinions cluster?
Three	Internal experts	What are the top-priority trends for competencies? What are they reading and scanning to influence their thoughts? What challenges will dominate here? What are the emergent problems and opportunities? Are there on-line collections of knowledge and wisdom that could serve as models? If so, are they relied on? Refreshed?
Four	Sponsor(s)	Report on stages one through three. Seek priorities.
Five	Job incumbents	What are the top-priority trends for competencies? What obstacles do they perceive? What will help them move in these directions?
Six	Survey	What are respondents' top priorities for growth, given what we have learned in prior stages? What obstacles do they perceive for their growth? What will help them move in these directions? See Table 6.6a, which represents the quest for priorities, and Table 6.6b, which seeks drivers.

Will this effort influence the status quo? How?

How is the source invested in the status quo?

If things change, how might their world be altered?

Have the sources been properly briefed by their leaders? By you?

Do they know why you're there and why they are being tapped for information, opinions, and access to materials?

What related efforts have occurred in the organization? How do they muddy the waters?

TABLE 6.6A. PARTIAL SURVEY FOR TRAINING AND DEVELOPMENT PROFESSIONALS.

Please rate priorities for your own professional development.

Description of Capabilities	For each item, circle the number that best reflects your priorities. 2 = Top priority 1 = A priority 0 = Not a priority *Your Priority*		
Serve the client and the organization			
1. Know where to go for information about what the customer needs.	2	1	0
2. Know what questions to ask and what materials to examine.	2	1	0
3. Know how to explain the analysis to assure organizational access and support.	2	1	0
4. Know how to use interviews, focus groups, and surveys to gather data.	2	1	0
5. Know what the data mean and how to explain them to the customer.	2	1	0
6. Know about the many ways that human performance can be improved.	2	1	0
7. Know how to explain the impact of individual and organizational root causes on human performance.	2	1	0
Develop and deliver solutions			
8. Know the attributes of effective instructor-led and independent learning programs.	2	1	0
9. Know how to develop effective training materials, for example, instructor guides, student guides, cases, and practices.	2	1	0
10. Know how to use a variety of learning technologies, for example, World Wide Web, CD-ROM, satellite, multimedia, and distance learning.	2	1	0
Measure impact			
11. Know how to build and pilot prototypes prior to rolling out the finished solution systems.	2	1	0
12. Know how to report results and revisions.	2	1	0

TABLE 6.6B. PARTIAL SURVEY TO MEASURE PRIORITY NEEDS AND ANTICIPATED BARRIERS.

Do the following statements reflect your situation, thoughts, or beliefs?

For each item, circle the number that best reflects your thoughts.

2 = Agree
1 = Neutral or Don't know
0 = Disagree

Statement	Your Rating		
1. I am in favor of the increased emphasis on technology-based delivery.	2	1	0
2. I need to know more about performance improvement strategies that go beyond instruction.	2	1	0
3. I have a computer that I use in my work.	2	1	0
4. I see benefits in moving toward more collaboration with cross-functional colleagues.	2	1	0
5. My manager is eager for me to demonstrate the skills, knowledge, and perspectives emphasized in this survey.	2	1	0
6. I think I'll be good at moving in these directions.	2	1	0
7. I am eager to learn more about the topics that are described in this survey.	2	1	0
8. If I begin doing the things on this survey, I will be recognized for these efforts.	2	1	0
9. I am willing to make the time necessary to develop my skills and knowledge in these areas.	2	1	0
10. My customers are eager for us to shift in these directions.	2	1	0

Let's look at typical performance analysis sources and make some assumptions about what their questions and concerns might be. I'm not suggesting that each of your sources will possess all or even any of these views and perspectives. Some surely will. Be ready for them and address their concerns at the get-go. It will improve both your relationship with the source and the quality of data that result from the interactions.

Table 6.7 illustrates some of the key concerns of *job incumbents* during performance analysis. Job incumbents are the focus of the effort. Anybody could be a job incumbent. Engineers might be; so could maintenance workers, human resources professionals, teachers, and executives.

Table 6.8 describes the perspectives that some *experts* bring into the interaction. I've included suggestions that are matched to their views.

Table 6.9 describes the perspectives that *managers* might bring into a performance analysis. Note the similarities with the hesitancies of the job incumbents.

Solution partners are the colleagues across the organization or working as vendors from outside the organization, with whom you might cooperate to ensure performance improvement. Compensation specialists, organizational developers, organizational effectiveness experts, reengineers, and information technologists are examples of solution partners. Their concerns would emerge after data about drivers have been gathered and you're attempting to bring the necessary professionals to the table to collaborate. Table 6.10 describes the perspectives that these partners sometimes bring into a performance analysis.

Executives come to the table with different issues. Table 6.11 describes some views executives might hold and offers suggestions for addressing their concerns.

Be Authentic

My trusty dictionary defines *authentic* as "genuine, true, reliable." Graduate students will often ask how they should handle one situation or another. Although specific suggestions vary with the circumstances, one consistent urging is to be authentic.

TABLE 6.7. JOB INCUMBENTS' PERSPECTIVES.

Incumbents' Perspectives	Analyst Strategies
The employee doesn't want to participate. Perhaps he avoids meetings. Or comes late. Or is unwilling to utter anything except monosyllables.	Remind him about the importance of the project. Describe positive effects on him, his unit, the work. Answer questions about who was selected, who you are, and confidentiality.
The employee wants to know why she has been chosen for these inquiries.	You can tell her one of three things: (1) you were randomly selected; (2) you were identified as a model performer (truth is important here—employees know if they're that kind of performer); (3) you were identified by X as having some important views on this matter.
The employee wants to know your credentials.	Share them. Note those elements with which the incumbent will identify. If he is an insurance agent, describe your years in the field selling insurance prior to this assignment. (No lies, of course.) Take a little time to explain your role, what you are seeking, the reasons you need him and others in that role.
The employee is unimpressed by your credentials.	Acknowledge that you haven't been an insurance agent or whatever. Describe how you've prepared for this conversation, indicating what you've read and with whom you've talked. Emphasize that you've come to her and other agents for their significant practical experience, which you admittedly lack.
The employee is concerned about being involved.	Why is he concerned? What might that suggest about the organization? This is where you make further assurances about the confidentiality of data and tailor your responses to the concern(s).
The employee isn't interested in helping out.	Why? If it isn't because of the issues already raised, then it might be that the employee hasn't been properly prepared to participate. Has the supervisor encouraged participation? Have you oriented the employee ahead of time and then again at the commencement of the meeting?

TABLE 6.8. SUBJECT MATTER EXPERTS' PERSPECTIVES.

Experts' Perspectives	Analyst Strategies
The expert enjoys the distinction and job security that comes from being the only one (or one of the very few) who knows. She doesn't see good reasons to share, as that will erode the monopoly.	Reiterate the importance of the effort. Explain how she will be credited in the effort. Detail ongoing relationships and expectations regarding her continued involvement with the effort.
This issue is a low priority for this expert. Maybe he's moved on to another project. Maybe he's never been very interested in the domain to begin with. Maybe he's turned off by past experiences, where he failed to receive credit for contributions.	Reiterate the importance of the effort. If the expert persists in avoiding contact or fails to provide necessary information, ask why. There are many possible reasons. Target your responses to the particular concern—for example, by defining credit issues or assuring him there will be follow-through. In a pinch, make certain that an executive sponsor has weighed in on the importance of this project.
The expert is so enthusiastic that she is ready to devote energy that far exceeds your plans for her.	Express appreciation for that enthusiasm. Identify how you hope to involve the expert, using tangible examples about meetings or briefings or reviews. If the expert is disappointed by the role, explain why it is defined as it is—for example, by explaining that engineers from other geographic areas need to be involved in order for the program to be widely accepted. Consider increasing her role. Why not?
The expert is concerned that *other* experts are going to be involved in defining the outcomes and subject matter.	Describe the many sources who are involved in defining any effective program: internal and external experts, the literature, model performers, and so on. Explain why broad participation in definition is beneficial if the program is to be widely accepted.

TABLE 6.9. MANAGERS' AND SUPERVISORS' PERSPECTIVES.

Managers' Perspectives	Analyst Strategies
The manager is acting uninterested in the effort. Perhaps she avoids meetings. Or comes late. Or is unwilling to utter anything except monosyllables.	Remind her about the importance of the project. Describe the benefits to her, her unit, the work. Note the priority that a sponsoring executive has attached to the effort. Answer the questions she has about who was selected, who you are, and confidentiality. (Also see below.)
The manager wants to know why he has been chosen for these inquiries.	You can tell him one of three things: (1) you were randomly selected; (2) you were identified as a model performer (truth is important here—employees know if they're that kind of performer); (3) you were identified by X as having some important views on this matter.
The manager wants to know your credentials.	Share them. Note those elements with which the manager will identify. If she is a regional manager, describe your years in the field and note any management experiences. (No lies, of course.) Explain why managers' and supervisors' perspectives are critical here.
The manager is unimpressed by your credentials.	Acknowledge that you haven't been a manager in the field. Describe how you've prepared for this conversation, indicating what you've read and with whom you've talked. Emphasize that you've come to him and other managers for their significant experience, which you admittedly lack.
The manager is obviously concerned about being involved.	Why is she concerned? What might that suggest about the organization? This is where you repeat assurances about the confidentiality of data.
The manager doesn't approve of the direction that your effort is taking the organization.	Why? Solicit his opinions. Don't debate. Capture his views. Report those views back to the sponsors without attribution.

TABLE 6.10. SOLUTION PARTNERS' PERSPECTIVES.

Solution Partners' Perspectives	Analyst Strategies
"You're who? This is novel. Why is some-body from _____ asking *me* to come to a meeting?"	Say something about the project and why it is a priority. Name the client or sponsor for the effort. Share the data that indicated it was important to involve this person (his skills, perspectives) in the effort. Seek his participation. Sell a systemic approach to the initiative.
"Why is a 'training' person doing something other than training?"	Explain that before you could do any training, it was important to find out what training had to be done. In that process, you found that there were other things that had to be done to fertilize the organization, or the training wouldn't matter.
"What's your role here?"	Explain that you're attempting to put the necessary people together. You're not the boss, just somebody who is attempting to make sure that the effort moves forward in all the necessary places.
"Does my manager know that I would be working on *your* project?"	Prior to inviting this person, make certain that his leaders are willing to play a part in this effort. It's possible that the sponsor or your manager will need to smooth the path here. Communication with leaders across the organization is important preparation for successful cross-functional collaboration.
"We're billable, as you know. Have you got the money for me to get involved?"	Use the same strategies as those immedi-ately above. You know if the organization operates like this. Will you need to arrange to "buy" internal or external expertise? Seek that support ahead of time.

TABLE 6.11. EXECUTIVES' PERSPECTIVES.

Executives' Perspectives	Analyst Strategies
"Thank goodness you're here. I've got to go to Singapore, and I need you to bring this one to fruition while I'm on the road."	If the executive is disappearing, who will play her role on this project? Your work as analyst needs to occur under the aegis of an executive or sponsor. Push back. The executive or another leader must be involved. The trick is to define a "reasonable" amount of executive involvement or to find a substitute sponsor.
"This is a tough one, and I'll want to see everything before it goes out. In fact, maybe we should meet daily."	This is the micromanaging executive. Why is he concerned? What's tough? Put some energy into gathering data on his views of the situation and then negotiating a close relationship that isn't oppressive.
"I'm concerned that your interactions with employees will stir things up in the field."	You are asking about drivers and barriers, about organizational consistency and messages. Explain why it is important to raise these issues and how you're going to use the data. Cite past efforts that were unitary and thus unsuccessful. Brief her regarding the solution system that will emerge. Offer the opportunity to review questions prior to your meeting with people in the field.
"Why is a human resources gal [or a training guy] talking about processes and software and organizational climate?"	Explain that you expect to be doing some training but that you want to customize and tailor the effort, which involves getting out into the organization. Does the executive want training events *or* improvements in the performance that he was talking about earlier?
"What role do you expect me to play?"	This is a good opportunity to make certain that the executive understands what it's going to take to be successful on this project. How can she help? What sources must be contacted? Will you draft a letter for her? What solution partners might be involved? How can the executive prepare people for collaboration on solution systems?

Why am I fussing about authenticity? The reason is that there is a tendency for fledgling analysts to think that there is one way to execute the stages and deliver the questions and dialogues presented in this book. I doubt there is. The words presented here are suggestive. They must be tailored to you and your situation. If you're effusive and enthusiastic, be that way. If you're quiet and measured, that's fine too. The key is to be prepared and consistent and—if your style and proclivities are causing problems in communications—to discuss them with the source.

For example, a colleague in the software business often drew quizzical looks from engineers. He is perky, eager, and emotional about projects. Most of his sources were less so and didn't immediately trust his enthusiasms. After my associate noted the difference between his style and that of his sources, allowed that his manner can take some getting accustomed to, and began to spice his conversation with citations and numbers, communication improved. He didn't stop being himself, but he toned his presentation down a tad, to give them a little more of what they expected.

Here's an approach to more authentic communications: first, I suggest that you *take a reading on your reactions, and monitor your feelings and thoughts.* It's easy to get swept away in the moment, when the expert refuses to help out, or the customer says that you will be signing a contract that forbids you from using or demonstrating the deliverable. Start by getting a handle on what you're thinking and feeling. For example, one of my students put it something like this:

> Well, I was coming off overly emotional on this. And I didn't want to do that. It makes me sound young and inexperienced. I calmed down and took my pulse on the situation. I really like this project, but I am getting a little resentful. I feel that my client ought to be more generous about letting me use this project afterwards. I'll put many hours into this effort, and I'm getting paid a pittance. OK, I'm overreacting. I want to be able to present at conferences, and this would be a great example. Shouldn't I be able to add this to my portfolio to strengthen my case for positions in the future?

Next, *ask yourself about those feelings and thoughts.* Are they reasonable? Can they be understood by the client or expert or colleague? How do your perspectives conflict or mesh with the other person's view? My student said, "[My client] could hear all of that—the parts about the effort and time and small remuneration. And I think he'll resonate to the part about my portfolio. Not sure about the conference thing. Might be a concern there. They're very serious about holding their examples and cases confidential."

Third, *make your case based on what you were thinking and feeling and your rational assessment of the other's perspectives.* Be willing to reveal concerns and priorities that are unique to you, mentioning your job hunt, for example, or your desire to show off your work at a conference. Rather than taking a general stand, such as, "I will work my fingers to the bone on this one and should be able to do with it what I want, especially since you're paying me so little," approach it more specifically and tangibly. Try, "As you know, I graduate in December, and I'm eager to be able to show prospective employers what I've done in graduate school. I want to do that at conferences and in interviews when I show my portfolio. I will be proud of the work done for you and want to include it."

Finally, *ask for help.* "How can we work this out so that I can use this effort for my job search and so you and your organization will wind up with a great project and be fully comfortable with our agreement?"

This approach would work just as well for an internal human performance professional who is trying to tempt a difficult expert into cooperation. Table 6.12 presents a similar example of authentic communications that highlights these four steps.

Remember That Performance Analysis Might Be Perceived as Threatening, Controversial, and Intrusive

Why would that be? The question takes us back to the kinds of information we gather during performance analysis. Let's start with a situation in which you are attempting to get a picture of directions, including optimal performance and perspectives, and of what's currently going

TABLE 6.12. AUTHENTIC COMMUNICATIONS.

Steps to Authentic Communications	What You Might Think or Say
Monitor what you're thinking and feeling. Ask yourself what you're thinking, how you feel, why you feel that way, and what else might be going on.	I'm incredulous. This woman was assigned to talk with me about team nursing and nurse leadership. Now she's stonewalling, or I think she's stonewalling. Dr. Isaacs said he'd set it up. I presume he did. I can't believe this. It's close to rude. And I hate to beg for information. This is awful. Get me out of here.
Take a tour of your ideas and feelings. Are they reasonable? How would the other person respond to your inquiries? Why might they see your questions differently?	Maybe I'm reacting a bit much to her lack of enthusiasm. Has Dr. Isaacs gotten around to explaining the effort to her and why she is important to it? Did he explain my role? *Is* she stonewalling, or does it just feel that way to me? She might perceive me as meddling in her ongoing project, whereas I see myself as helping to spread her view of the approach throughout the hospital. Could she be concerned that I won't give her credit for her work?
Make a case that includes your perspectives and hers. Tell her why this matters to you; include carefully selected elements that reveal your priorities.	"Why don't we back up a bit? Did Dr. Issacs tell you about this project? I get the sense that maybe you haven't been included up front in all of this, that you need for me to start from the beginning. You are one of the nurses who is heading up the hospital team leadership concept. You're actually doing it, and from what Isaacs says, you're doing it in a way that they want to spread across the organization. I'm here to learn from you. I'm hoping that you will provide key definitions for us and a clear view of where the barriers might be. I'm not a nurse, but I've done quite a bit of work on teaming and team leadership. We might have a lot to offer each other."
Ask for help on this.	"Can I answer any questions you have? I want us to work together on this. Without you, it's hard for us to tailor this important program to our hospital."

on. If we are seeking to know what excellence looks like in a "broad stroke" kind of way, some experts or model performers might hesitate about sharing their secrets or views. If they reveal what they know to you, what impact might that have on their unique position in the organization? And if you turn around and package their wisdom for wider dissemination, wouldn't their contribution become less rare and special? Whereas you as a training and development professional may be participating in the current thrust toward organizational learning and sharing, some employees are more compelled by the waves of workforce reductions.

What else could threaten? Maybe the expert isn't an expert and doesn't want it recognized. Maybe the expert doesn't want to share ownership. Or maybe the expert is unwilling to invest time in collaborating with other experts from other countries or regions. Or perhaps the expert prefers to talk to other experts and recognizes that you aren't one.

Your work as a performance analyst also involves capturing a view of current performance. That might concern people in the organization. If you're reviewing sales figures, scrap production, and customer feedback, somebody is going to worry about what you're finding out about individual contributors. If you're asking people what they do, how they carry out processes, about their successes and failures, this too might evoke concern. They'll wonder, why are you asking? Why are you asking *me?* Why are we talking about my unit and people?

The same concerns arise when you get into the quest for drivers and barriers, only more intensely. Here you are going beyond documenting what's happening to inquiring about underlying causes. This rivets attention in a big way. The concerns frame up like this: Did somebody suggest that I'm responsible or that our group is responsible? Is there some perception that we're not getting it done? Why would you be talking to me about this? Will what I say be repeated? What are other people saying about this?

There are no simple solutions here. Find out what's causing the glitch in communications and tailor your responses. Which human and organizational concerns are pricked by your appearance? Table 6.13 presents some suggestions for addressing your sources' most loaded concerns.

TABLE 6.13. THREATS TO COMMUNICATION.

Type of Concern	Suggested Approaches
Concerns relating to **optimals:** ownership of expertise, willingness to share, job security, collaboration with other experts, exposure of the absence of expertise, and so on	Focus efforts on defining the relationship, including the expert's or model performer's ongoing relationship with the effort. Note credit that will be received. Note executive sponsorship. Acknowledge the concerns of the expert. Match your approach to the particular concerns.
Concerns about **outsiders knowing what is going on** and about who or what might be **factors driving the situation**	Acknowledge reasonable concerns about revealing this information to others. Explain why you have been assigned to this project. Describe similar past efforts and how you have in the past and will in the future maintain total discretion regarding the data.
Concern about **confidentiality**	Acknowledge legitimate concern about confidentiality. Focus on how the data will benefit this source. Detail strategies you will use to maintain confidentiality. Explain that you will never attribute quotes and opinions. Identify similar past projects in which you have successfully maintained confidentiality and individual privacy.
Concern about your **lack of expertise**	Admit that you aren't an expert (unless you are). Explain that you are talking to this person or this group for that very reason. You need their wisdom about the topic or the context. Detail the methods you've used to prepare yourself to make good use of the time your sources are giving to this effort. Review documents and literature in advance so that you can cite your preparatory efforts.

Ask your source about his or her concerns. Identify and articulate them. Admit that you empathize with his or her view and hesitations, and then offer rejoinders matched to those concerns. Make your case for participation based on your past efforts and projects.

Emphasize Planning

Take nothing for granted. Assume that every interaction, from an interview to a focus group to a survey, succeeds because of preparatory effort.

Become clear about your purposes. Are you seeking directions through inquiries about optimals? Are you looking for a fix on what's going on? Are you seeking opinions on drivers for performance? Note that these purposes will serve as the generators for your questions. The early chapters of this book and Tables 6.2 and 6.5 detail sample purposes and questions.

In addition to these substantive purposes, note that you are always on a mission to win friends for your organization and for this effort in particular. That's a critical aspect of any and all front-end work. You're looking for information *and* allies. You cannot do it alone. You want executives who understand and sponsor the mission; incumbents and supervisors who know where the organization is heading; experts who leave their fingerprints all over your plan; and colleagues from sibling organizations who will unite with you in a performance improvement system.

Review appropriate materials. What can you review? What publications or documentation can you read prior to interacting with this expert engineer or developing the survey? You should not only read in advance but also make certain that what you learn shapes and enlightens your efforts. You might say, for instance, "As you know, I'm not a software engineer, but I am fluent on the prior system and spent a couple of hours reviewing the technical specifications for the new one. I have a pretty good idea of where we're going in this version. What I need at this point is your view of the prior rollout and your ideas about what we can do to ensure more success in the future."

The cover letter or paragraph for a survey might include the following: "As you look at the list below, you might wonder about where we got this list of competencies. Recently I've interviewed people in our organization and reviewed reports provided by the two major engineering professional associations located in Washington, D.C. We have combined the information derived from these various sources to create what you find here. Now we want your reactions to possible directions for the future."

Consider the likely perspective that sources will bring to the table. This chapter posits many outlooks that sources might hold (as detailed in Tables 6.7 through 6.11). Don't be surprised by what you find. Preparation includes contemplating the viewpoints of the people you are asking to help with the effort and planning how you will recognize and respond to their concerns.

Establish a plan for each interaction, including introductory communications, agenda, and follow-up. Let's take a look at these sample communications.

A voice mail message to an *external* expert might sound like this: "Agatha, this is Nosilla Stone in human resources at North American Technologies. We met a few years ago when I was working on our Call Center customer service project. Well, we want to revisit that effort and would like to get you involved. It wouldn't entail huge amounts of time from you, maybe five to eight hours over the next month, but we'd need at least two hours in the next week. Our questions focus on new approaches to customer service and strategies to put those programs in place. We know what we've got now, but we'd like to get your view, a view that we hope includes what other state-of-the-art efforts look like. Can we work that into your schedule?"

An e-mail message to an *internal* expert might look like this:

Dear Vicente,

    Mick told me he discussed the customer service project with you and that you're expecting this e-mail.

    What I want to do here is to give you a little background on the project and to get your thinking about what we'll be discussing on Tuesday at 3, in your office. By the way, I really appreciate your involvement in this. You've been very successful with moving your group in this direction, and the whole organization needs to learn from what you're doing.

Well, that's it. We're going to ask you what you're doing, in some detail. How did you influence customer service improvements? Your organization had the same training everybody else did. Why did it result in so much change for the better? If you've got any particular memos or policies that you wrapped around the prior effort, will you please bring them to the meeting? There's some thought that the supervisors are key players in this initiative. Will you please think about their roles at your site?

Mick and the Council decided to take on the topic of customer service because we continue to get a steady stream of complaints and lukewarm opinions. Except from your area. That's why I need to know more about how you and your folks are handling it.

Again, thanks. See you Tuesday at 3.

The agenda for the meeting with Vicente could be e-mailed to him in advance of the meeting or presented when you appear. An agenda is important because it establishes leadership and keeps the discussion on task. Exhibit 6.1 is a sample agenda for the session with Vicente. Note the use of time-certains.

Some follow-up is appropriate. It can be as slight as a thank-you e-mail or as grand as a letter, with a copy sent to Mick, and a set of minutes from the meeting. Let's look at what might be sent to Vicente by e-mail. Minutes or a note that documents the interaction are valuable as a tool to revisit what occurred, to prod promised actions, and to serve as a record of the event.

Hi Vicente,

Thanks for the time you spent on the customer service project last week. I think we made good progress.

We agreed that you would serve as an ongoing member of the Planning Committee, a group that will probably meet three more times over the next eight weeks. We also agreed that you would play some role in the work that we do with managers and

EXHIBIT 6.1. AGENDA FOR A MEETING WITH AN EXPERT.

AGENDA
Customer Service Initiative
September 9, 1999

Participants: Vicente Mata, Mesa Superstore;
                Nosilla Stone, Human Resources and Training

Goals: (1) To familiarize Vicente Mata with the project;
          (2) to provide background about the effort;
          (3) to learn about the current successful effort at the Mesa Superstore.

3:05   Describe the background of this project, including data on the
        prior service effort and results.

3:20   Discuss potential roles for Mr. Mata in the upcoming customer service
        effort.

3:30   Discuss the following questions: What did the Mesa Superstore do
        prior to and as follow-up to past customer service training? What does
        Mr. Mata perceive to be the supervisor's role in this effort? What are
        he and the store doing now to ensure continued performance? What
        ways might their efforts be strengthened? To which employees should
        Ms. Stone speak for their perspectives on effective customer service?
        What are the logistics for arranging to meet with employees?

4:00   Discuss future collaboration and next steps.

supervisors. It might be briefing, training, or even appearing as an expert in video clips we might be producing. One good possibility is for you to serve as an on-line coach for chats and discussion groups that we think we might be rolling out with the project. As you can see, our exact plans are still being hatched.

You promised to dig out the supervisor checklists that you distributed to your people after the workshop. Please send them to me as soon as possible. We're going to consider adapting them for the entire organization.

I'm still working on a document that details the four key components of your customer service effort. I'm putting the description and the materials you provided together into a comprehensive package; I'll send it to you before I forward it to other committee members. I want to make sure it reflects your views.

As I promised at the meeting, I discussed your ongoing involvement with Mick. He was delighted, and appreciative. I am too.

I'll be back to you about subsequent meetings. Now, I'm off to meet with that external expert I told you about. Tomorrow, I meet with four of your supervisors. And thanks for setting that up.

CHAPTER SEVEN

WHAT TECHNOLOGY CONTRIBUTES

Ayesha: Did you get this e-mail? Look at this—it's a survey about our parking policies. You know, I think we might use something like this to get a handle on the customer service program, maybe to do the up-front study with the reps and the customers?

Gus: But don't you think our people would be resistant? They prefer face time, I think.

Wendy: This company is supposed to be a high-technology place. Look at our products, where our profits are coming from. I think we ought to be looking for ways to reach out to people through technologies. And more and more of our employees, and customers, are global. There are downsides to the technology, of course, but I'll bet there are more pluses.

In this chapter, we examine what technology can contribute. We'll tour e-mail, the Internet and Intranet, videoconferencing for data collection,

Mark Fulop and Rebecca Vaughan, graduate students at San Diego State University, contributed to this chapter.

and software for data analysis. What follows is a discussion of technologies linked to the priorities and concerns of colleagues like Ayesha, Gus, and Wendy.

Using Technology to Collect Data

Considering that many employees now have access to e-mail, with others joining up every day, how might we use it for planning? E-mail can be used to conduct interviews, gather expert opinions, and conduct electronic surveys and virtual focus groups.

Interviews via E-Mail

The dominant use of e-mail in performance analysis is for one-to-one asynchronous communication, which is especially useful for contacting experts and model performers. The professional can ask for opinions about how to handle a situation, what the policy is, the reasons for a new approach, key areas of pain and gain, and how the source perceives the situation.

When collecting opinions about the work or problems with it from selected sources, e-mail is appropriate. For example, via e-mail, Mark Fulop interviewed a VP for marketing at a software and consulting firm about his uses of e-mail. Mark reports: "Over the course of three e-mail messages and a 'hard copy' postal mailing, I was able to build an understanding of how technology could better match individual employees with work challenges and how it could be used to track performance improvement. My . . . access to the VP of a company on three occasions was made possible by e-mail." If you can cultivate responses, and that is a big IF, e-mail is a good way to find out how key sources think and feel.

There are other advantages to e-mail. Consider the global reach of e-mail. You need that reach if your expert on customer loop design or disaster mitigation is in Singapore or London and you're in Frankfurt or Foxboro.

Then there is speed, especially compared with snail mail. And there is also the electronic record of the interaction, available for subsequent reference and analysis. If you cast a wide net via e-mail, it is very useful to have a repurposable electronic record of the results.

Another benefit is the control the respondent has. Late night? No problem. Dawn? No problem. Holiday break? No problem. Your respondent can consider your queries when she wants to, even if you transmitted them to her and the other engineers in the middle of the night. This provides flexibility that overcomes the vexing challenges of getting calendars together, often across vast distances and time zones.

The respondent's control of the situation also relates to the constraints associated with the use of e-mail for analysis. Respondents reached via e-mail may choose not to respond at all, especially if you're not there to make an impassioned case for it. Another impediment is that key informants are sometimes unversed in the uses of e-mail or without access to it. A final concern about e-mail is the lack of spontaneity. Respondents are able to hatch responses they think will please, and they might tend to do so, because they know that their "signed" responses are a record that others *could* see.

The benefits of anonymity, of course, are not readily available in e-mail. E-mail users know it is easy to forward and store messages. Would you share your feelings about current performance problems and their causes if you thought they might get routed or touted? There is no simple answer here, but it will help a lot if you send an e-mail message that alerts respondents to your coming query, responds directly to their anticipated objections and concerns, assures them about your oath of confidentiality, and reminds them *why* the effort is important.

Focus Groups via E-Mail

E-mail can also be used to gather perspectives from large numbers of people. You can use e-mail software to build group distribution lists for memos, newsletters, and other correspondence simultaneously directed at multiple recipients. This is particularly appropriate for gathering perspectives on priority goals, what is going on currently, and what performance drivers are or might be. Performance analysis questions (for example, Which of the following do you see as contributing to the error rate?) can be widely distributed, with speed and at low cost. Distributing questions and receiving responses, both of which might take weeks using conventional mail or days using phone or fax, can be hastened with an e-mail distribution network.

Will the members of the electronic group honor you with honest data? Will respondents volunteer opinions if there is the danger that they can be known to many at the tap of a keystroke?

There are two remedies here, neither of which is a perfect fix. One is to earn a reputation for maintaining the confidentiality of your sources. Promise it and deliver it. Establish a record of never attributing data to its source, except in a secure way (for example, "A veteran analyst in the Asia-Pacific region"). The other remedy is to use a technology that routes all responses through a box in the system that removes any distinguishing marks and characteristics. If you're in a paranoid environment, one buffeted by reductions in force, for example, your assurances must be strong, clear, and truthful—and bolstered by technology.

Electronic Surveys via E-Mail

Another strategy to gather opinions is to use e-mail surveys. Although hard copy surveys are not a typical means to gather PA data—because their history shows them to be anything but swift—e-mail can bring surveys into the fold as an apt approach. A growing body of literature supports the use of e-mail in survey research (Thach, 1995; Mehta & Sivadas, 1995; Kittleson, 1995).

An important benefit of e-mail surveys is their ease of rapid dissemination to a given group; you don't have to spend time and resources reproducing surveys, stuffing and addressing envelopes, and waiting and hoping for responses using global or national postal services. Researchers (for example, Thach, 1995; Mehta & Sivadas, 1995) have found a bonus in the quality of responses to e-mail. E-mail surveys, they believe, tend to result in more insightful and candid responses. Although the reasons for this are unclear, Thach posits that survey respondents might perceive more social distance than in traditional communication situations and therefore offer more reflective and less careful opinions.

In 1995, two researchers at the University of Cincinnati, Raj Mehta and Eugene Sivadas, surveyed hundreds of users of twenty popular Internet discussion groups. Five random groups were established; two received traditional mailed surveys, three received e-mail surveys. The survey methodology for the five groups differed in other ways as well, because the researchers were also attempting to examine the importance of incentives and pre- and post-survey notification. The group that was offered a $1 incentive to complete a mail survey had the highest response rate (83 percent), followed by the two e-mail groups (one with no incentive, the other with pre-survey notification).

Some questions linger about the effectiveness of e-mail survey response rates; the literature presents a mixed picture. But response rates are only part of the picture. Mehta and Sivadas's study demonstrated that the costs were lower and the response time faster for the e-mail group surveys. And the survey responses were similar across groups for completeness and response substance. The researchers found that e-mail groups wrote significantly more than the snail mail groups, leading them to suggest that the quality of e-mail response provides a compelling reason to use technology for open-ended inquiries.

Unlike people responding to printed surveys, which benefit from anonymity, e-mail respondents have good reason to be concerned about the traceable trail of e-mail. Will the quality of the data be hampered by the absence of privacy and confidentiality?

The best solution here relates to prior notification, a topic I touched on earlier. Intruding into a person's e-mail with a survey that has not been preceded by an explanation is not a good idea. Mehta and Sivadas (1995) tangled with this barrier in their research. One of the groups in their study received surveys without warning, and because of the number of complaints from this group, the researchers aborted their participation.

A supportive strategy I mentioned earlier is to use "stripper" boxes. Electronic responses are sent to a neutral box that provides the automated service of removing all identifiers. Then the "stripped" version is forwarded to the person conducting the electronic survey, with a copy to the respondent that demonstrates how all designations have been removed. Again, prior communication is critical here, with respondents and the organization's Management Information Systems (MIS) unit.

Set up the system. Explain the system. Explain why the survey is important. Provide a way for the participant to see how the automated system works. And express appreciation for the time that the respondent is donating to the effort.

Time and foresight are also continuing concerns. You're already behind the eight ball if you commence your study *after* somebody calls to ask for a class or for help with a human resources problem. The customer is more likely to be frantic than reflective. You can work around this harsh reality by *anticipating* where leaders are taking the organization.

Begin seeking performance analysis information early and often. Use electronic surveys regularly to seek priorities about directions for your efforts. Play a part in the conversations and planning in the organization. For example, several of my graduate students are involved in this kind of anticipatory effort for a company that builds and repairs ships. What are the emergent needs of the electricians? Of the paint and blast people? There is no request for a particular intervention, just the desire by human resources professionals to find out how employees and their supervisors see their development needs. This is what I mean by virtual analysis (also discussed in Chapter Five): the professional *continuously* takes the pulse of the organization and its people, actively contributing to its direction. This can be accomplished in traditional modes or via e-mail queries and electronic discussions that reach out into the organization in systematic and habitual ways.

Using Technology to Nurture Ongoing Dialogue and Collaboration

More and more, human resources and training professionals are being asked to serve as leaders in creating learning communities in their organizations. A global pharmaceutical company provides an example. Suppose the leadership wants to support their chemists worldwide in continuous professional growth and collaboration with colleagues from other, related disciplines. How do they accomplish that? How do they contribute to increasing interdisciplinarity and reducing organizational silos? What can be done to turn experiences with customers, clients, products, and the literature into archives of lessons for their associates from other disciplines? What role can human resources leaders play in knowledge management? Technology in the hands of human resources and training professionals has much to offer here.

Discussion Groups

Discussion-group software anticipates the challenges of knowledge management through discussion groups and automated distribution lists. These software packages are referred to as listservs, majordomos, or listprocs. In a sense they create a virtual post office that distributes e-mail to the addresses of participants in a defined group. The group might be engineering managers, affirmative action officers, members of the customer service unit, people passionate about distance learning, or customers who have purchased a particular printer. Routine administrative tasks are automated, and the software archives messages for future reference. The software typically enables a moderated group, in which messages are screened prior to distribution, or an unmoderated approach, with no prior screening.

Anticipate the challenges of the future and begin structured dialogues on those topics. What skills will people need to adjust to *global* teaming? What issues and opportunities are emerging for petrochemical engineers during their deployment in the former Soviet Union? What are the implications of object-oriented programming for the technical community? What about the implications of objects for the education and training community? How can the top two hundred executives in a large global organization better use the Web for strategic planning? What are the current barriers to integration of technology into the sales process? Plant questions like these within internal or external electronic discussion groups and enjoy the flowering of discussion. Then initiate programs to address the concerns and opportunities that emerge, or hold the data for when a request is presented.

Videoconferencing

Another technology that enriches the ongoing conversation is videoconferencing. Computer networks are increasingly being used to transcend the flat, linear nature of e-mail or voice telephone with the introduction of electronic whiteboards and videoconferencing. The basic concept behind videoconferencing and computer whiteboarding is that computers with inexpensive mounted cameras can deliver not only text but also audio and visual images in real time. In addition to the video image on the screen, participants can view and manipulate a shared text window. This is a whiteboard; shared viewing of it enables us to make changes and save the collective results. These evolving technologies allow groups to collaborate in real time across geographic distances.

Figure 7.1 lists a few technology resources. Before you purchase anything, please examine these options in light of new options that might be more appropriate for your situation.

PictureTel, a videoconferencing firm, offered a case study about their technology at 3M (1996). At the time of the effort, 3M, with eighty-five thousand employees, had more than fifty major product lines. 3M turned to PictureTel videoconferencing to help it understand far-flung customer needs and to connect its teams to meet those needs. According to PictureTel, videoconferencing technology allowed 3M to create a virtual research lab in which teams collaborated despite being thousands of miles apart. ProShare is another key player in the videoconferencing arena. White Pine, makers of CuSeeMe, is releasing a group conferencing software, MeetingPoint. And Microsoft has recently released NetMeeting, software with promise for collaboration and shared data, soon to become standard fare in Microsoft's offerings. Several associates give NetMeeting rave reviews.

I used videoconferencing as part of the front end for a management development project for a medical equipment company. Although it did enable us to keep participants on both coasts involved in the effort and

FIGURE 7.1. PARTIAL LISTING OF SOFTWARE FOR ANALYSIS.

Company	Address	Telephone	Web Site	Product
Videoconferencing Resources				
AT&T	32 Avenue of the Americas New York, NY 10013-2412	(800) 828-9679	www.att.com	Vistium 1300
Compression Labs	350 E. Plumeria San Jose, CA 95134-1911	(800) 225-5254	www.clix.com	Cameo
Intel	P.O. Box 58119 Santa Clara, CA 95052-8119	(800) 538-3373	www.intel.com	Proshare 200 Video System
PictureTel	100 Minuteman Road Andover, MA 01810	(800) 716-6000	www.pictel.com	PCS 50
White Pine Software, Inc.	542 Amherst Street Nashua, NH 03063	(603) 886-9050 (800) 241-7463	www.wpine.com	CuSeeMe MeetingPoint
Magna Publications	2718 Dryden Drive Madison, WI 53704-3086	(800) 433-0499	www.distance-educator.com/vcs.html	Distance Education Report (on-line journal)
Statistical Software Resources				
SPSS Corporation	444 N. Michigan Avenue Chicago, IL 60611	(800) 543-2185	www.spss.com	SPSS for Windows SPSS for Macintosh They make a less expensive "gradpac" limited version for students.
SAS Institute	SAS Campus Drive Cary, NC 27513-2414	(919) 677-8000	www.sas.com	JMP Statistical Discovery Software
Abacus Concepts, Inc.	1918 Bonita Avenue Berkeley, CA 94704-1014	(510) 540-1949	www.abacus.com	StatView

FIGURE 7.1. PARTIAL LISTING OF SOFTWARE FOR ANALYSIS, *continued.*

Company	Address	Telephone	Web Site	Product
Statistical Software Resources, *continued*				
Minitab, Inc.	3081 Enterprise Drive	(800) 448-3555	www.minitab.com	MiniTab DOS and Win (easy to use)
	State College, PA 16801-3008			
Texasoft	P. O. Box 1169	(800) 955-8392	www.texasoft.com	Winks Professional Ed. (easy to use)
	Cedar Hill, TX 75106-1169	(972) 291-2115		
Research Triangle Institute	3040 Cornwallis Road	(919) 541-6000	www.rti.org	SUDAAN
	RTP, NC 27709			
Qualitative Software Resources				
Researchware Inc.	20 Soren Street	(617) 961-3909	members.aol.com/ researchwr	HyperRESEARCH (Win and Mac)
	Randolph, MA 02368-1945			
Sage Publications, Inc.	P.O. Box 5084	(805) 499-9774	www.sagepub.com	NUD*IST
	Thousand Oaks, CA 91359-9924			
Qualis Research Associates	PO Box 2070	(413) 256-8835	www.qualisresearch.com	The Ethnograph
	Amherst, MA 01004			
HyperQual	3327 N. Dakota			HyperQual2 (Mac)
	Chandler, AZ 85224			

briefed about analysis results and future plans, the experience wasn't always as smooth as silk. We suffered occasional technology glitches that mucked up free-flowing communication. And there is always concern that the meter is running on long distance phone charges. The technology has great promise, however, especially as improved and Internet-based options appear.

Internet Alliances

Human resources planning can be enhanced by electronic participation and bonding that extends beyond any one organization. Whatever the concerns are, it's likely that other performance professionals are thinking about them too. Affiliation with professional groups on-line keeps you alert to the requests that are just around the bend. Figure 7.2 describes some professional options for on-line affiliation.

A useful listserv is the Discussion Group for Training and Development (TRDEV-L). Approximately five thousand subscribers from sixty different countries exchange information on training and development. Real problems and people populate the listserv. This listserv is often used

FIGURE 7.2. PROFESSION-BASED ON-LINE DISCUSSION GROUPS.

Liszt, The_Mailing List_Directory, enables you to survey many possible groups. Check out http://www.liszt.com/

The Learning Organization (LEARNING-ORG) was founded by Richard Karash and is dedicated to those interested in organizational learning.

Subscribe by sending an e-mail message to this address: majordomo@world.std.com Include as the message: info learning-org

The Discussion Group for Training and Development (TRDEV-L) was founded and is tended by David Passmore. It is dedicated to those working in training and development.

Subscribe by sending an e-mail message to: listserv@psuvm.psu.edu Include as the message: sub trdev-l your name

Lakewood Publishing hosts a Web site that has more than two hundred related Web addresses. Visit http://www.trainingsupersite.com

Another interesting site is Jim Kinneer's site devoted to FAQs in our business. Visit www.microserv.net/~jkinneer

as a forum for gathering opinions: "How do I prepare managers to receive their first dose of 360-degree feedback?" "How do I bring automation to sales people?" "How do I learn more about electronic performance support?" "Has anybody read anything good on the subject of performance analysis?" Many fruitful responses result from these kinds of queries. One caution, however: buyer beware. Most groups are open to anyone who wants to join.

Using Technology to Handle and Present Data

Because technology makes it easier to generate data, it can add to the professional's burden. What do you do with all the data? What do the data mean? How do you make sense of them and then make a case with them?

Fortunately, technology can assist here too. The paragraphs that follow provide a swift tour of the options. Consult with experts in the organization who specialize in crunching data. Take out your old statistics text, or better yet, visit a nearby university. Contemporary research classes will introduce you to software that helps analyze and represent data.

Quantitative Data

Software can help us understand large numbers of responses to quantitative questions with speed and ease. Figure 7.1 lists several prominent software packages. More are becoming available every day. Just this morning I found a Web site that specializes in assessment instruments. (See http://www.questionmark.com/ for one example of the rich resources popping up on the Internet.)

Let's set up an example. Imagine that you are the performance consultant to a large engineering group. The executive for that group, your customer, wants help in finding out why the engineers get such lousy reviews on the engineering briefings that they make within the corporation and to external customers. What can be done to improve their efforts? She was hoping that a training class on "presentation skills" would take care of the problem but is willing to hear what you think ought to be done, based on a speedy analysis of the situation.

As part of your performance analysis, it makes sense to find out what the engineers are thinking about impediments to their successful briefings. One way to do it would be to describe the executive's concern to the population of engineers ($N = 200$) in a preliminary e-mail message. In this first short note, you describe the issue and solicit their participation, informing them that you'll be asking for their ideas soon. A few days later you send the e-mail message presented as Exhibit 7.1.

The data summarized in Figure 7.3 show that the chief problem areas, averaged across all engineers and departments, and listed in order of decreasing magnitude, are as follows:

G. Giving a good briefing doesn't count for anything.
J. Engineers are the wrong people to do the briefings.
D. Engineers are pulled away from their real work by the briefings.
C. Engineers don't know how to do briefings and speeches.

Qualitative Data

Not all data are as readily quantified. Responses to open-ended questions from surveys, interviews, and focus groups present a different and greater challenge for data analysis and presentation. What do you do with that second question in the e-mail message in Exhibit 7.1? ("If you had the power to improve the engineering briefings, what would you do? Please take some time to describe what the organization might do to improve the briefings.") This kind of question seeks subjective or qualitative responses. They help us to understand what's going on with the people and the organization.

How does one begin to tell the story and draw the pictures from this data? Typically, the data collector pulls out tape, scissors, and highlighters and begins the tedious process of cutting and pasting and coding the documents based on common themes and ideas. Hours later, pictures and stories begin to emerge.

EXHIBIT 7.1. E-MAIL LETTER.

Dear colleagues:

When I wrote to you late last week, I told you that Ray Trahn and the Executive Engineering Council are eager to seek your opinions about ways to strengthen the engineering briefings. I'm sending you this e-mail message because we want YOUR opinion. If we are to improve engineering briefings, the opinions of engineers must drive our approach.

What you say will be held in strictest confidence. When I report these data, they will be aggregated, reflecting what groups of people recommend, not the beliefs or statements of any one engineer.

Please take a few moments to respond to these two questions now. It should take about five minutes. I'll expect your answers within 48 hours of the time and date on this message. And I'll be back to you with the results. Thank you in advance.

Put a number at the end of each of the options below. Rate EVERY option, please, and return this message to me.

2 = a major factor   1 = a factor   0 = not a factor

1. As you know, we are attempting to improve the quality of the engineering briefings. Why do you think the briefings are not appreciated by customers?
   A. Engineers aren't given sufficient time to plan the briefings.
   B. Engineers don't care about doing the briefings.
   C. Engineers don't know how to do briefings and speeches.
   D. Engineers are pulled away from their real work by the briefings.
   E. Engineers aren't good at those kinds of activities.
   F. Engineering supervisors don't encourage the briefings.
   G. Giving a good briefing doesn't count for anything.
   H. The people who give the good briefings aren't usually the best engineers.
   I. Engineers don't know how to plan the briefings.
   J. Engineers are the wrong people to do the briefings.
   K. Customers are the ones with the problem. They don't get technical content.

2. If you had the power to improve the engineering briefings, what would you do? Please take some time to describe what the organization might do to improve the briefings.

FIGURE 7.3. QUANTITATIVE SURVEY DATA.

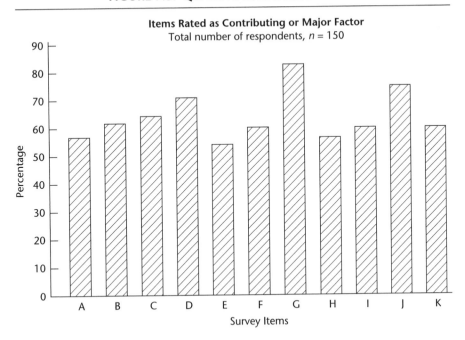

Software for qualitative analysis is an electronic facilitator of text-based analysis, helping the researcher to parse the data and explore relationships between responses.

Let's explore the subject of qualitative research by looking at something a researcher actually did, and on a topic of interest to us. Imagine that you were working in a company that was considering moving from a traditional, instructor-led training environment to a laboratory in which individual employees would be given time to be actively involved in their own learning. How would you determine which of the two approaches achieved greater results? This was the question that Ian Hart of the University of Hong Kong was asked to answer (Hart, 1997). Hart compared a lecture format and a computer lab problem-based format for a building construction course. In order to assess the effectiveness of the individualized, problem-based learning lab over a period of eighteen months, the project employed (1) video recordings, (2) individual and group interviews with students, (3) standardized tests, (4) drawing of concept maps, and (5) systematically collected student work.

Given this abundant quantitative and qualitative data, the challenge was analysis. Hart chose the qualitative software research tool NUD*IST. During iterative analysis, he coded text using that software package to create categories; over time, the quantity of coded text, video, and evaluations allowed Hart to begin to explore the meaning of the data. Among Hart's conclusions was that the problem-based approach supported more complex cognitive thinking by students.

Our engineering example provides another opportunity to witness the uses of technology during analysis. Sixty engineers chose to respond to the second question posed in Exhibit 7.1. It is interesting to note that the engineers' qualitative perceptions about what to do are consistent with the top factors they reported in response to the quantitative question. Consider also the impact of an open-ended question on the response rate. Out of 200 surveyed, 150 engineers completed forced-choice question one, but only 60 completed the more open-ended question two. The compelling data, however, justify the inclusion of that question.

In the original e-mail message, we promised that we would be back to the engineers with the results. One way to do that is via e-mail, as illustrated in Exhibit 7.2. Using technology to swiftly share results is an excellent way to build support for the current and subsequent efforts.

◆ ◆ ◆

This chapter surveys the role technology can play and already does play in performance analysis. Options available at the time of this writing will no doubt be expanded or enhanced. By the time you are reading this chapter, much more is certain to be available.

Focus attention on the basic challenges we face in performance analysis: reaching sources, collecting data, understanding data, and making data understandable to others. Table 7.1 summarizes the possibilities and reviews the terrain covered in this chapter.

Revisiting the definition of performance analysis from Chapter Two, we see that the speed, cost-effectiveness, and all-around efficiency of these

EXHIBIT 7.2. FOLLOW-UP E-MAIL LETTER.

Dear Colleagues,

Last week I reminded you that Ray Trahn and the Executive Engineering Council are concerned about the engineering briefings. I sent you a short survey asking for your opinion on why the quality of engineering briefings is declining and what you think should be done to improve them. Thanks to all of you who completed and returned the surveys. We got a good mix of participation from engineers in all departments with a wide range of experience in the company. Your insights and suggestions will be very helpful to Ray and the council in their efforts to improve the briefings.

As I promised, here's a quick overview of the results:

- When asked why you think the engineering briefs are not appreciated by customers, the top four factors were as follows:

Factor	Percentage of respondents saying this is a contributing factor
1. Giving a good briefing doesn't count for anything.	82
2. Engineers are the wrong people to do the briefings.	74
3. Engineers are pulled away from their real work by the briefings.	70
4. Engineers don't know how to do briefings and speeches.	64

- When asked what you would suggest to improve the briefings, here's what you said:

Percentage of responses	Solution	Illustrative quote
47	Someone besides engineers should do the briefings.	"Engineers aren't good salespeople. We're good at what we do—let us do it! Leave the briefings to those with good people skills, like the project managers."
32	Provide better tools or support for engineers who do briefings.	"The customers don't seem to like our presentations. Either they don't care, or we're over their heads—too technical. We could use some sort of template or list of important points that the customers really want to know."
15	Provide proper incentives for engineers who do briefings.	"No one seems to appreciate that we do these briefings. It just seems like more work with no reward. In fact, we get just the opposite—more pressure because we get behind in our work when we have to do these briefings."

Thanks again for your help. If you have any questions regarding these findings, feel free to contact me by e-mail or by phone.

TABLE 7.1. SUMMARY OF TECHNOLOGY FOR PERFORMANCE ANALYSIS.

The numbers below reflect the ways that technology can serve performance analysis.

1 Collecting data from sources 2 Group processes 3 Data analysis 4 Communicating results 5 Optimals 6 Drivers

	1	2	3	4	5	6	Key Advantages	Key Disadvantages
E-mail interview	•			•	•	•	Asynchronous nature allows greater access to experts Allows user control Stores responses in text format Provides access to optimals from experts, stars	E-mail overload Loss of interpersonal dynamics Cannot guarantee confidentiality Hesitations about responding
E-mail discussion and focus groups		•		•	•	•	Bridges geographic and time barriers Provides access to field experts and SMEs Builds group identity Produces extant data for future mining Supports partnering and goal definition Fertilizes the environment by educating the organization on future trends	Some difficulty in determining quality of sources Uneven responses and participation No confidentiality—people take a public position
E-mail survey	•				•	•	Is inexpensive and speedy Bridges geographic barriers Allows wider participation Can yield high-quality responses	Concerns about confidentiality Thus, concerns about data quality Response rates?
Data mining			•	•	•		Repurposes existing data Seeks lessons from past and implications for future	Assumes quality in existing data Usually involves large, organizational commitment

	1	2	3	4	5	6	Key Advantages	Key Disadvantages
Professional listserve	•			•	•		Maintains professional currency Provides way to test ideas and benchmark	Who are the sources? What is their credibility? Why are they taking the positions they take? Can be inundated with information and opinions Caveat emptor
Internet videoconferencing and whiteboard		•	•		•		Bridges geographic barriers Allows for real-time interaction Data are captured in text form Screen sharing can focus attention and save money Emergent programs, such as NetMeeting, offer accessible possibilities	Technology access is limited Bandwidth is still "narrow" in many settings Relatively complicated with "glitches" Telephone costs can be high
Statistical software			•	•			Automates statistical analysis Represents data visually	Must know what to ask the software to do for you Packages can be costly
Qualitative software			•	•			Standardizes coding of qualitative data Allows for hypothesis generating and limited testing	Can be time-consuming to code large amounts of data Limited data-analysis options

various technologies support the performance consultant: *performance analysis (PA) is partnering with clients and customers to help them define and achieve their goals. PA involves reaching out for several perspectives on a problem or opportunity, determining any and all drivers toward and barriers to successful performance, and proposing a solution system based on what is learned, not on what is typically done.*

Let's look at several elements of this definition of PA to see how technology could help Ayesha, Gus, and Wendy (the participants in the dialogue that opened this chapter).

• Partnering. By fostering internal e-mail discussion groups, Wendy can anticipate her clients' needs and stay in touch with current organizational issues. By interacting with her clients on a continuous basis, she can also help them define their goals.

• Several perspectives. Easy access to people and data allows ongoing data collection from a variety of sources, whether in Boston or Bangladesh, automatically producing data for future "data mining." Ayesha can draft an occasional e-mail to customer service representatives or customers to get a sense of their opinions about the on-line support for the new product line.

• Not typically done. Being involved in external professional listservs allows you to explore future trends and possible solutions from others in the field. Gus may turn to a listserv to find out how he can get his people to "warm up" to technology. You can also use technology to capture large numbers of dispersed opinions and to present them in ways that compel.

Technology supports several "mantras" highlighted in this book:

• Be systematic. Technology supports you in an iterative process, that of collecting data from one phase and using it to focus subsequent questioning and data-collection efforts in the next phase.

• Manage the project. Technology helps you perform an essential duty as a responsible project manager: *staying on time and within budget.* For instance, e-mail allows you to swiftly initiate activity, "nudge" key sources, and monitor ongoing processes. Digital interactions also create instant records of decisions and plans.

• Avoid analysis-paralysis. Shave time off the front end and avoid paralysis by continuously "checking in" with key players and getting quick turnaround when testing your hypotheses. You'll keep the project on track and ensure more buy-in when solutions are rolled out.

CHAPTER EIGHT

COMMUNICATING RESULTS

Margie: I did it. The performance analysis took just over a week, even with all the other things I had to do. Plus I read some background materials over the weekend when I started it. Now comes the challenge of making a case for what I found. I'm concerned because my interviews and scan of the literature suggest it's a bit more complicated than the self-study course that they want me to build.

Ana: Well, it's a good idea to put some effort into the way you bring your recommendations forward. I've had some experiences with my customers not appreciating my results as much as I did. I thought I had ferreted out some mind-boggling things, real surprises, and then the executive committee wouldn't go along with my recommendations.

Margie: Sometimes the studies confirm their opinions and directions, and then it's no problem at all. But usually, when I get a chance to dig into it, the analysis reveals more than was expected or something altogether different. That makes reporting trickier.

What can we do to increase the likelihood that our findings will be appreciated and acted on?

There's much we can do. In this chapter, we'll look at several ways of sharing results, highlighting those that can be done in small and informal ways and those that require a somewhat grander effort.

How and When Do We Report?

Let's look at how and when we report. Table 8.1 is a summary of the possibilities.

There are a few aspects of Table 8.1 that deserve emphasis:

• Report throughout the process. People in our business sometimes are guilty of trying to be saviors for their customers. Some are inclined to take a request for assistance and run with it. Our customers—many of whom will eagerly wash their hands of the situation, given the opportunity to do so—may encourage this sort of behavior. The customer is, in essence, asking us to wave a magic wand to meet his or her needs, whether that need is customer service or contemporary skills and perspectives for hospital administrators. Although we might be eager to delight our customers with sorcery, sorcery is pretty much what it would be, if we attempted to go it alone, without their involvement. Successful performance initiatives involve concerted efforts installed and nurtured close to where the work gets done. The executive who wishes to toss people over to training to get them ready for the new global initiative or who expects human resources to change the forms so that appraisals will improve is headed for disappointment sooner or later.

We report throughout the process so that the customers are brought along. They hear about how many of their managers are concerned about X. They see that the errors, in the view of the engineers, are primarily being caused by Y. They review unattributed quotes from job incumbents that show the complexity and texture of the situation. From beginning to end, they should be looking at snippets of the data and conversing with you about what those might mean. Avoid surprises. This is no time to pull a rabbit out of a hat for customers. They won't

TABLE 8.1. REPORTING OPPORTUNITIES.

When We Report	How We Might Do It
To keep the customer posted on progress, results, what-not, *throughout the process*	E-mail message with appropriate attachments Informal conversation or meeting Memo with appropriate attachments Formal oral briefing
To involve the customer in a discussion and reflection on what you're learning	Informal conversation or meeting Formal oral briefing and work session
To request specific assistance with some portion of the effort, such as garnering time from an expert or executive	E-mail message Informal conversation or meeting Memo with appropriate attachments
To seek more access to sources	Informal conversation or meeting
To report data back to those who served as sources	E-mail message Memo Oral briefing
To communicate with colleagues across the organization about results and to secure their interest and involvement	Informal conversation or meeting Oral briefing
To communicate results and recommendations	Oral briefing with supporting displays and appendixes Report with supporting appendixes

like the rabbit. They'll discredit the hat. Involve customers in the performance analysis throughout, because sharing increases the likelihood that customers will understand the data and help determine their implications. Customers are more likely to enact recommendations that they participated in hatching.

• Inform sources about what their contributions mean to the effort. When you visit organizations, it's typical to hear strong sentiments regarding participation in studies: "What for? It doesn't make any difference what we say." "What for? They ask us so they can *say* they asked us. They already knew what they were going to do."

The only way to counter this accumulated cynicism is to make sources' contributions mean something. Report back to them. Share selected results about key questions. Provide them with some quotes and solicit their reactions. Share a brief list of the ways that their perspectives are going to influence the initiative. I'm not suggesting that you distribute your final report to all or that you visit many groups and offer oral briefings. You will achieve more credibility if you communicate frequently and in short, pointed bursts. The follow-up e-mail letter in Chapter Seven (Exhibit 7.2) is one example. Those engineers can see that their efforts will soon turn into action.

• Report to your customer *and* to others who might be involved as a result of the performance analysis. Share what you're learning with the sibling HR providers we've talked about throughout this book. It might be the folks in information technology, or your colleagues in compensation, or the management development team, or the specialists who manage selection, or the process reengineers who are reworking the sales quality effort, or. . . . They are members of your organization, although typically they are not within the same unit.

You're confronting the realities presented by "otherness," or organizational white space, as Geary Rummler and Alan Brache would talk about it in their fine book, *Improving Performance: How to Manage the White Space on the Organization Chart* (1990). While you're working on the sales project, your associates around the organization aren't giving it much thought. It's *your* project. Or it's your *group's* project. Your potential collaborators typically reside in another group or unit; it is likely that they march to a different drummer. You can't assume that these colleagues are going to jump on board just because your study suggests that the effort requires their contributions. Sharing the effort and data with siblings and their leadership is critical if a solution system is to be installed as a result of the performance analysis.

• Show your customer that you have a handle on the situation and clear ideas about how to proceed. This is the opportunity to present what you've discovered with related recommendations. Describe what you did; what you found, in the words and opinions of your sources; and what you think it might mean. Present options for where to go next, as well as any potholes that concern you. Tone is important here. This is your opportunity to make a case for the direction(s) you want the customer to select.

The emphasis here is on process, data, multiple ideas and options, and data-driven support for your recommendations. Your customer might have expressed a requirement to you this way: "The performance appraisals look perfunctory to me. Can't we do something about this?" Table 8.2 provides an example of one way you could summarize findings.

• Although clarity and command are good, some circumstances call for more finesse and less masterfulness. Some clients want you to provide strong direction. They sought your expertise and expect you to demonstrate it. In those cases, tell them what you found and what you think they ought to do. Be sure to include your rationale, based on the data from your analysis. Table 8.2 provides an example. Here you put your recommendations on the table and seek concurrence and support to move the effort forward. Focus on those areas that you see as essential to the effort and invite discussion of those approaches that are more "iffy." As shown in Table 8.2, you might want to discuss the benefits of an on-line database. Or you might wish to solicit your client's ideas about ways to show that the executives *really* mean it this time.

You could, however, be more tentative and inductive about it. That's appropriate when you have a client eager to talk about the implications of the data and to participate in the process. A recent client of mine in the transportation business is a good example. Telling him what to do would not have worked. No matter how sound the recommendations, from the get-go he wanted to be involved in hatching the solutions. When this is your situation, provide the involvement. Our clients and customers are the only ones who are in a position to turn these suggestions into action. We need them to believe in the outcomes of the performance analysis. They are more likely to if they play a role in figuring out what the data reveal.

It's simple to shift to this more involving and open-ended approach. Looking again at our example in Table 8.2, just take the right-hand column. Present those data and ask the client what he thinks they mean, whether they are important and what strategies might be effective, given the information. Share quotes and numbers. If the client is uncertain about how to handle an element of the data, then step forward to

TABLE 8.2. SAMPLE RECOMMENDATIONS FOR IMPROVING PERFORMANCE APPRAISALS.

Recommendations	Rationale
Create an on-line database for the twenty most frequently identified areas for performance improvement linked to local and corporate resources for addressing these problem areas.	A review of eighteen randomly pulled appraisals found that only four had credible improvement strategies. Just under half of the supervisors were able to generate appropriate suggestions about what the employee might do to improve performance.
Rewrite the personnel policy to reflect executive commitment to honest appraisals, support for development, and support for managers who do the more difficult thing.	The personnel manual has eight pages detailing the employees' grievance rights and procedures and two-thirds of a page about the rationale and value of performance appraisals. One supervisor said, "Look at page two; look at pages four through thirteen. The story is there. There's no real commitment to appraisals that mean anything!"
Work with human resources to create a recognition program to honor supervisors who bite the bullet and coach and develop their people via the appraisal system.	Thirteen of fifteen supervisors agreed or strongly agreed with the statement "I don't think the company *really* wants us to do anything with these appraisals."
Conduct a short briefing for supervisors that communicates the new commitment to appraisals. Highlight changes in policies and strategies to support managers who identify problems and work at them.	One supervisor said, "Look at page two; look at pages four through thirteen. The story is there. There's no real commitment to appraisals that mean anything!"
Provide a training program that addresses the communications strategies appropriate to constructive feedback and employee development. This strategy should be enacted *after* the organizational interventions listed above.	Just over half of the supervisors admitted that they didn't know how to deliver anything other than good news to employees. Only three supervisors said they were very confident in this area.
Acknowledge past flaws and inconsistencies in the appraisal program and create a communications program that describes the new, aligned effort.	

present possibilities. In this approach, it's important to come to the client prepared to share a formed view of what you think is required. But rather than laying it all out on the table (as in the left-hand column of Table 8.2), you're going to engage in a discussion focused on the data from the right-hand column.

Three Reports for the Same Customer

Let's look at several related examples based on a short, targeted performance analysis for a people development challenge. I'll set the stage: one day, a director of performance for a consulting firm called and asked for help. Just a few months before, his title had been "director of education." Now, with a new title that reflects more the future than the present, he rules the performance improvement domain. This domain is populated by sixty people with such titles as instructional designer, CBT developer, Web-based information specialist, and project manager. The director's job was to lead these able professionals as they shifted their practices and perspectives to include performance improvement concepts. The director was convinced that his associates had to know more about performance improvement so that they could do it and talk about it in a way that would sell services and programs to customers.

What follows are three reports associated with the effort. The first, shown in Exhibit 8.1, is a brief, written report that was submitted at the end of the study. Exhibit 8.2 is a facsimile of the Microsoft PowerPoint slides and notes associated with the presentation to the original customer and a few of the managers with whom he works closely. Finally, you'll get to see something that is a little different. Exhibit 8.3 is a draft of a briefing for our customer to edit for his use in reporting these results to upper management.

Now let's look at the oral briefings associated with this study. Exhibit 8.2 attempts to make clear recommendations *and* to solicit opinions. As you can see from the hard copy report (Exhibit 8.1) and the slides and notes in Exhibit 8.2, it isn't unusual to do *both* a report and a briefing with visual support.

EXHIBIT 8.1. BRIEFING REPORT.

Introduction

The challenge presented by the director of performance for Traincomm 2000 (T2), a training-product development and consulting company, was to help determine what needed to be done to support the movement of his organization, composed of sixty professionals in two locations, from training to performance consulting services. Although T2 does not intend to abandon the development of training media products, they wish to expand the array of services and systems they provide to their customers, focusing particularly on customizing their responses, rather than on selling inventoried services. The director is concerned that the history of media product development is getting in the way of a smooth transition. He said in his charge, "I think we're doing pretty well, but I know we all have a tendency to hang on to the familiar. We've been great at the media side of things; we need to be great at this expanded role."

The purposes of the performance analysis were to

- Seek the opinions of the people doing the work about the expanding role and performance improvement, in general
- Identify organizational and individual drivers to success
- Determine priorities for professional development
- Incorporate all these opinions, and those from the literature and benchmarked organizations, into a proposed solution system

We reviewed the literature on performance consulting and the shift from training to such consulting. We conducted thirteen confidential interviews of approximately thirty minutes in length; ten were with performance technologists, and three were with project managers. We conducted one focus group with five professionals, including instructional designers, project managers, and a graphics artist. Although participants were chosen randomly, three interviews and one focus group member were opportunistic. These individuals were in proximity when the randomly selected interviewees were unable to partake.

The Idea Is Acceptable

Ten out of thirteen interviewees said the shift from training to performance consulting was a good idea. The three who hesitated either lacked information or expressed muted acceptance of the concept. Those in the focus group generally agreed that this shift was likely to be good for business. Most made it clear that they readily appreciate the value of performance improvement and performance development. Representative and typical comments were as follows:

- "I like the idea of providing our clients with a whole solution, not just a training program."

- "We shouldn't provide a solution before knowing what the problem is, so I support the analysis stuff, always have."

- "This is an opportunity for us to grow."

- "It makes sense to have a more holistic picture and to get out of the box business."

The Staff Is Confident

The group is noticeably confident. Six of the interviewees and nearly everybody from the focus group said they were very confident in their ability to thrive in the new situation. Six others said they were confident or somewhat confident. Reasons for their confidence included three interviewees' holding advanced degrees in related areas, a belief in their own abilities, and the support they enjoy from peers and managers. However, one manager and a few people in the focus group stressed the need for staff to develop new skills to avoid the tendency to fall back on doing things that are known, familiar, and comfortable. This matches the perceptions of the director.

Drivers to Success

The people at Traincomm generally agreed about how to approach this transition.

More Definition of the Role and More Communication About It

Six performance technologists asked for guidance about competing priorities and for a more specific definition of their emergent role. One interviewee said, "Give more clarity about this job. I understood it when we were making media programs and could point to a beginning, middle, and end. Now it's not so clear, especially when the managers talk about ongoing relationships and customer development." Another asked, "What are the expectations of a performance consultant?" Still another pointed to all the stand-up trainers and production people and the need for collegial relationships with them. She was concerned about the overlap and reminded us about the billability the company currently enjoys from these classes and media product sales. The manager from the focus group expressed the need for guidance on how to coach a performance-oriented team. He felt that the criteria were "murky, unclear. I can't always tell when they're on point and off." This manager asked, "What are some appropriate kinds of performance goals that I could suggest for my employees? And how do I modify my performance evaluation system to match?"

EXHIBIT 8.1. BRIEFING REPORT, *continued.*

Time Is a Concern

Although several professionals from both the interviews and the focus group expressed a desire for skill development, almost all respondents were concerned about allocating time to such development, given their current workload. One focus group participant said, "We should think about our needs in the same way we're being asked to do for our clients. We need some sort of 'just-in-time' support instead of training consuming our time." One veteran was interested in an electronic performance system to which they could turn for assistance without going to classes. The majority saw good reason to make development a priority and expressed no resistance to classroom instruction.

Perceived Need for More Participation

Four interviewees felt more directed than included in decision making. One said, "Too often we get dragged in after the decisions have been made." Two interviewees and the manager from the focus group urged the use of a team approach to share the benefits of what is learned by the units and individuals. One interviewee and several focus group participants were keen on formalizing the sharing of best practices across units. A manager said, "So many great tips and techniques are lost from project to project—I see it all the time."

Customer Education and Communication About Performance

There was strong concern about the readiness of their long-term clients for the shift to performance. "Sure it sounds great, but my customers don't know about it. They come to us for CD-ROMS or video-based courses, and now some Web stuff. The trick is to bring them along on this performance thing."

Several performance professionals from the focus group were concerned with educating external customers: "Most of my clients see us as a training vendor that does classroom training or CBT." One manager emphasized the need for materials to support staff as they attempt to explain performance improvement concepts and services. One interviewee said, "Can't we use our marketing and graphics folks to help us explain this new thrust in plain English? Just look at this skimpy brochure."

Seven interviewees mentioned that the rest of the company lacked an understanding of what performance professionals bring to the table. They "got" what the product group did, but not this more amorphous performance concept. Respondents urged top management to more directly communicate how performance consulting can benefit the entire organization and to work with the staff to produce materials that enable everyone to come up to speed on this effort. One professional worried that the rest of the company would omit the group from its contracts if they "don't have a clue about what we're up to."

Priorities for Training

One interviewee suggested that training should be more than classroom experiences; he wanted the program to model uses of emergent technologies. Still another interviewee agreed that it was important to constantly try to identify needs and bring skills to the team, suggesting that whatever is done ought to be part of an ongoing system.

As part of the analysis, respondents were asked to rate a short list of items as a top priority for training (2 points), a priority for training (1 point), or not much of a priority for training (0). The original list was derived from the literature. The list below shows the items and the total scores received. Although the numbers offer up some obvious distinctions—for example, that performance and needs analysis and selling the approach are top priorities, and history and instructor-led training are not—be careful about investing too much importance in tiny numerical differences. What these numbers do is provide a general impression of where participants think development resources ought to be concentrated.

Performance and needs analysis	41
What a performance consultant does and could do	35
Theoretical and historical foundations of performance consulting and performance development	11
Specific interventions:	
Selling a performance and system approach to customers	47
Selling a performance and system approach in the organization	40
Emergent technologies and their implications for performance	36
Feedback systems	30
Independent learning programs and materials	27
Job aids	24
Selection and staffing	20
Incentives and rewards	20
Job design	14
Organization design	13
Instructor-led education and training	8

Additional priorities for training added by the interviewees were computer literacy, project management, change management, instructional design, information mapping, evaluation methodologies, coaching, Web-based performance support, and on-the-job training.

EXHIBIT 8.1. BRIEFING REPORT, *continued.*

Recommendations

What follows is derived from interactions with nearly one-third of Traincomm 2000 performance professionals, the literature, tales from benchmarked organizations, and experiences in other settings.

Training is important but not sufficient to effect the shift.

☞ A generally confident group would become even more confident with development experiences in the areas they identified: performance and needs analysis; strategies for marketing and customer education; and emergent technologies for performance improvement. Other priorities are feedback systems and independent learning.

Whatever is done for customers should also be done here in the organization. Model a solution-system approach to performance improvement.

☞ Establish a recognition program related to training and performance improvement outcomes.

☞ Establish an advisory group to discuss, debate, make concrete, and revise a definition of the performance professional. Develop materials that communicate the concept to external customers and internal colleagues.

☞ Institute a strategy for formal and informal sharing of best practices.

☞ Use emergent technologies to expand classroom instruction through Intranet-based synchronous and asynchronous interactions and collaborations.

☞ Create a Web site that crystallizes the professional development experiences and provides tools, templates, and take-aways for reference.

☞ Create a Web site or space on a fileserver to serve as a repository for examples of successful performance improvement efforts.

Focus on real problems and practical solutions.

☞ Make certain that each development event includes an opportunity for participants to practice on real-world, pressing Traincomm 2000 challenges.

☞ Establish pilot cross-unit collaborations to solve selected, common problems.

Create a communications program about this effort.

☞ Develop materials in several modalities that define performance concepts for customers and provide examples of T2 expertise.

☞ Create an electronic record of results, based on measures of performance and customer satisfaction, that can be used to make a case to customers and colleagues. Professionals are most eager for a repository for best practices.

Consider changing the name of the company.

☞ As long as the company is called Traincomm, customers and employees are going to think that training is the name of the game.

Conclusion

There is no sense of a desperate need for training so that performance professionals can do their jobs. Most perceive that they are doing them reasonably well, and there is no customer feedback to suggest otherwise. Because it is the director who is concerned, it is critical for him to begin working with the group to establish more clarity about expectations and high standards.

On the whole, the professionals expressed enthusiasm for their continuing professional development, resonating particularly to topics that are at the core of performance improvement practice, although there was some concern about time away from their assignments and the press to remain billable.

We hope that the organization will choose to advance its people through formal education and training and to move forward on the other proposed initiatives. It is the combination that will turn any development effort into enhanced performance for individual professionals, the larger organization, and the customers they serve. It would be a travesty to do training on performance concepts without aligned organizational supports.

EXHIBIT 8.2. REPORT TO THE DIRECTOR OF TRAINCOMM 2000.

The Shift from
Training to Performance:
Where to go . . . How to get there?

A Performance Analysis
for Traincomm 2000 (T2)
Performance Improvement Group

PRESENTER'S NOTES

This project began with a request from the director of performance at Traincomm 2000. Apparently the organization is shifting from its role as a vendor of training to an expanded role as a provider of performance consulting services. The question is, Where do we want to go? How do we get there?

In today's briefing, we will present the findings from our performance analysis and provide you with a set of recommendations. In general, our findings parallel your original thoughts on the matter, but they also provide some strong caveats about ways to approach this transition.

The Charge for the Project

- Changing customer demands lead to an expansion in our mission from pure training products and services to performance consulting.

- Employees must expand established expertise in education and training media products into uncharted territory.

- Uncertainty exists regarding where our professionals currently see themselves in regard to their competence and growth as performance improvement professionals.

- There is a desire to provide quality professional development opportunities to all employees in the organization.

PRESENTER'S NOTES

This shift is affected by a variety of factors in the organization's environment. In addition to making this shift, the organization wants to provide ongoing professional development.

EXHIBIT 8.2. REPORT TO THE DIRECTOR OF TRAINCOMM 2000, *continued.*

Purposes

- To determine **factors** that may hinder or facilitate success in the performance improvement realm
- To determine **priorities** for professional development
- To recommend an **integrated solution system** for T2

Methods

- Review of relevant literature on performance consulting
- Individual interviews with ten practitioners and three managers
- Focus group with five professionals
- Examination of current T2 policies and related communications

---

PRESENTER'S NOTES

Purpose
The solution system includes both individual and organizational systems that must be in place to increase the likelihood of successful implementation.

Methods
Of course we took a systematic approach to the effort. In other words, we considered a variety of sources and perspectives in developing our recommendations.

- We reviewed the literature on performance improvement, including Stolovitch and Keeps; Gayeski; Rummler and Brache; Rosenberg; Rossett; Harless; and Dean. You all have these references in our report as Appendix B [not included in this exhibit].

- As you can see, we wanted to capture the opinions of the people actually doing the work, so we conducted several interviews and a focus group.

- We also reviewed existing documents in your organization, such as the brochure you now distribute to customers about performance improvement, and current policies and job descriptions.

Performance Technologists Support the Shift

PTs think it is good for business.

- "I like the idea of providing our clients with a whole solution system, not just a training program."
- "It makes sense to have a more holistic picture and to get out of the box business."

Performance technologists see the shift to a broader array of services as an opportunity for professional growth, a good thing in and of itself.

PTs are confident and eager to accept this new role.

- Sense of support from peers and supervisors
- May require support in acquiring new skill set

PRESENTER'S NOTES

A majority of participants were very positive about the shift and appreciate the value of performance improvement for both themselves, T2, and their clients. They see this shift as an opportunity for growth and are enthusiastic about the challenge.

The group we interviewed was confident.

They are confident, but keep in mind that many still expressed the desire to polish their skills and keep abreast of new trends in the field. HPT takes them into some new areas, and they want help to become proficient in those domains.

EXHIBIT 8.2. REPORT TO THE DIRECTOR OF TRAINCOMM 2000, *continued.*

However . . .

Fuzzy performance expectations

- Establish the concept of performance consulting for T2
- Clearly define new roles and responsibilities
- Provide downtime for professional development
- Sponsor teaming and sharing
- Note that customers are unfamiliar with change and find approaches to this challenge
- Communicate how performance can benefit T2
- Provide PTs with help in communication
- Update T2's image from old to new via concerted program

PRESENTER'S NOTES

The group voiced several concerns, mostly with how they would perform under the current organizational situation. However, no one thought these challenges were impossible, and they all had robust ideas and suggestions for how to effect the shift.

Clarifying the Goals and Roles
This was a major concern. The organization needs to make clear the goals and the changes in roles brought on by the shift, not only to members of the organization but also to external and internal customers.

Teaming
PTs want to feel that they are being included in the decision making. Also, they would like to formalize the sharing of information and best practices across units and are concerned that great techniques are lost in the system and continuously reinvented.

Priorities for **Training**

What exactly performance consulting is and **how to sell** this new approach to customers

Specific performance interventions

- Emergent technologies
- Feedback systems
- Self-directed learning programs and materials
- Job aids
- HPT interventions
- Instructional design skills, with emphasis on analysis

Practical teaming skills, such as project management

PRESENTER'S NOTES

As part of the interviews and focus groups, participants responded to questions that asked them to rate their priorities for training. You have a complete breakdown in your report. Here are the top priorities.

Selling it. How to sell the approach to external customers and within the organization (their biggest concern).

Emergent technologies. Not only their own computer literacy, but how emergent technologies can be used in a performance system.

HPT interventions. Organizational development interventions such as selection and staffing, incentives and rewards, job design, change management, and organization design.

Instructional design tools and interventions. Specific design techniques such as information mapping, evaluation methodologies; new interventions such as coaching and on-the-job training.

EXHIBIT 8.2. REPORT TO THE DIRECTOR OF TRAINCOMM 2000, *continued.*

A Solution System That Makes Sense

Provide rich training experiences
- Provide practical experiences, real-world problems
- Include performance analysis, marketing and customer education, emergent technologies

Model a solution system throughout T2
- Establish system of knowledge management, including database of examples of best practices
- Use technology to expand classroom experience, crystallize knowledge commodity

Model commitment and communication through highly visible efforts
- Establish repository of successes for promotional use
- Revise the brochure so that it communicates!

PRESENTER'S NOTES

As you can see, employee feelings and priorities match nicely with the organization's goals. There seems to be a simple logic that follows from their concerns to their suggested interventions.

In fact, our experiences in other organizations and from the literature suggest a solution system that will fit nicely with the goals of both the T2 leadership and its employees.

Model HPT

Teaming and empowerment. Form a team with broad representation to establish a clear definition of the performance professionals' roles. Get team members to establish performance goals and to develop an incentives and rewards system to recognize achievement of these goals.

Technology. Create an on-line learning environment with synchronous and asynchronous interactions and collaborations. Create a Web site that provides PTs with job aids, tools, templates, and take-away references. Maintain a database containing examples of performance improvement success stories.

Visible Commitment

Opportunities. Encourage employees to work in teams to solve pressing, high-priority challenges.

Marketing. Communicate shift in priorities through internal and external marketing. Consider changing the name of T2.

Next Steps

Get visible support for solution system from upper management

- Share findings from performance analysis with VPs
- Communicate their sponsorship and priorities throughout T2

Establish task force to clarify goals and roles for performance consulting at T2

- Involve upper management and performance professionals
- Share findings from performance analysis
- Get customer input

PRESENTER'S NOTES

Although it's obvious that the director is gung ho on this project, we must ask about the existence of a high-level sponsor who will publicly support systemic interventions such as those proposed here. How can we help you, the director, sell your ideas to a vice president?

Next, you will need to complete further analysis into the details of exactly how to make the shift from training to PT. You may want to show your commitment to team involvement by forming a group made up of a few instructional designers, performance technologists, project managers, and an upper-level sponsor like yourself. This group can start to establish some company policies regarding performance technology and determine priorities for training and other intervention efforts. This team may want to involve an external client to gain that client's input on customer expectations. A good project might be the revision of job descriptions and the creation of an appropriate brochure for internal and external customers.

There's never too much we can do to help clients make good use of the work we do for them. Our briefing (Exhibit 8.2) is tailored for the director and several of his direct reports, but we also wanted to help this director make *his* case to the leadership. That's why we built a model presentation that he could edit for executive consumption. Should the director have been able to do this on his own? Of course. We wanted to make it easier for him and to help him swiftly communicate the messages to the leadership. Producing the kind of presentation shown in Exhibit 8.3 helps you focus on the customer's situation. Also, this reporting template increases the likelihood that your work will move off the shelf and into the mainstream of the organization.

Note that the visuals in Exhibit 8.3 remind the executives about the effort and attempt to nudge the leadership into alliance with the director of performance. The director is also encouraged to solicit suggestions from upper management.

Briefing the Customer About Engineering Briefings

The engineering communication challenge we explored in Chapter Seven provides us with a fourth reporting example. As you may remember, the vice president for engineering is concerned about the quality of briefings that engineers are offering to customers. She asks for help in determining what to do. That commences the performance analysis. Exhibit 8.4 shows a facsimile of the slides and notes for the final presentation to the customer. Note that the problem isn't solved after this PA. Rather, the study suggests that further interaction with customers and strategic planning are necessary prior to settling on the solutions.

◆ ◆ ◆

Reports come in many flavors. There are written reports and oral reports. There are various degrees of formality associated with reporting, ranging from dropping by for a moment or jotting an e-mail note to presenting lengthy, appendix-supported documents and making full-dress presentations to organizational leaders.

EXHIBIT 8.3. DIRECTOR'S REPORT TO THE EXECUTIVE.

The Shift from
Training to Performance:
What Do We Do to Make It Happen?

**Report on the Performance Analysis
for Traincomm 2000 (T2)
EVP of Human Resources**

The Charge for the Project

At our meeting on November 6th, we discussed progress on the expansion of our services into the performance improvement realm.

We solicited external help to give us a fresh view and to provide an example of a performance analysis.

Findings are generally congruent with the need to develop our people in this area *and* to provide more organizational supports for the shift.

EXHIBIT 8.3. DIRECTOR'S REPORT TO THE EXECUTIVE, *continued.*

Purposes of the Analysis

To see **how we're doing** on the shift, in the view of the people who must make it successful

To determine **factors** that hinder or facilitate success

To determine **priorities** for professional development

To recommend an **integrated solution system** for T2

Revisiting the Reasons for Expanding Our Strategy

Focus on client need—*valued outcomes*
- **Partner with clients** to serve their best interests
- Provide **data-driven** recommendations and **bottom-line** business results

Do the *right things*
- Define solution systems—**driven by causes,** not habits
- Put client and T2 resources into **the right things**
- Make certain our staff knows about an array of interventions **beyond instruction**

Develop a *systems perspective*
- Be aware of **performance context**—changes in one area affect others
- **Focus on alignment** within organization

The New Approach Isn't So New!

HPT is familiar and comfortable for our people.

- Systematic methods
- Opportunity to continue to build training and information products, *plus* . . .

Our people support the shift to performance roles.

- They value the approach for T2 and clients: "It makes sense to have a more holistic picture and to get out of the box business."
- They welcome the professional development and express confidence.

How Do We Make the Shift?

A Solution System That Makes Sense

Rich training interventions

- **What** exactly performance consulting is and **how to sell** it to customers
- Skills in emergent interventions, such as reengineering and technologies
- Knowledge management and sharing best practices

Nontraining interventions

- Model a solution system at T2
- Clarify PT roles, create communications program for clients, establish system of knowledge sharing, update reward structure to match shift from selling to making boxes?
- Others?

EXHIBIT 8.3. DIRECTOR'S REPORT TO THE EXECUTIVE, *continued.*

Next Steps

Reaffirm support and priorities

- Communicate these priorities throughout T2

Establish task force to clarify goals and roles for performance consulting at T2

- Involve upper management, performance professionals
- Share findings from the performance analysis
- Build a database of our performance successes
- Define the role and develop a communications package to share it with internal and external customers
- ?

EXHIBIT 8.4. BRIEFING ABOUT THE ENGINEERING BRIEFINGS.

Performance Analysis: What's to Be Done About the Engineering Briefings?

For SemiCon Devices

Executive Engineering Council

EXHIBIT 8.4. BRIEFING ABOUT THE ENGINEERING BRIEFINGS, *continued.*

Purpose

To determine requirements of both SemiCon and its customers regarding engineering briefings

To determine factors that may be hindering optimal engineering briefings

To recommend the individual and organizational systems at SemiCon that must be in place to ensure engineering briefings that are well received by customers

---

PRESENTER'S NOTES

This project began with a request from the executive council to look into what's causing poor engineering briefings. Today's briefing is to present preliminary findings and to gather your opinions in determining our next steps.

Goals for Today

Review findings from the preliminary data collection

- Customer complaints
- Interviews
- Survey

Capture SemiCon opinions and priorities based on data collection so far

Discuss the next steps and project time line

PRESENTER'S NOTES

We'll discuss our methods for data collection up to this point. We'll present findings from several sources. And we'll present some of our thoughts and ask you to please share your comments and suggestions.

EXHIBIT 8.4. BRIEFING ABOUT THE ENGINEERING BRIEFINGS, *continued.*

Nature of the Challenge

"People skills are perhaps the most difficult area for engineers to improve as they move into a project management position. . . .

Interpersonal skills often spell the difference between success and failure."

Thornberry (1987)

PRESENTER'S NOTES

This quote puts a little light on the issue. No doubt people skills is an area of performance that is somewhat foreign to the engineers. They're being asked to step outside their comfort zone a little. We're faced with an important challenge.

The Charge for the Project

Increasing market pressures to focus on customer service

Unique challenges that come from expecting technical people to play expanded customer-education roles

Uncertainty regarding where current engineers and supervisors currently see themselves in regard to their ability to brief and educate

Desire for leadership to examine and commit to a systematic, systemic, and data-driven approach to enhancing client relationships and improving customer satisfaction

---

PRESENTER'S NOTES

We know that this concern with engineering briefings is influenced by many factors in the organization's environment. We know that it's important both to look at the situation systemically and to collect data from a variety of sources in a systematic manner.

EXHIBIT 8.4. BRIEFING ABOUT THE ENGINEERING BRIEFINGS, *continued.*

What We've Done Thus Far

Review of relevant SemiCon documents, including customer comments on briefings

Interviews with randomly selected engineers and managers

Survey via e-mail of all engineers in company

Feedback to engineers regarding preliminary findings

Final report and briefing

PRESENTER'S NOTES

Here is a brief look at our systematic data-collection efforts thus far. We've completed the first four items on this list. You'll be seeing in detail the findings from our review of records, interviews with engineers and supervisors, and a survey sent to engineers.

Customers Aren't Satisfied

1. Briefings have an inappropriate focus.

   "These engineers just keep talking in technical terms. Frankly, that doesn't mean a thing to me. I just want to know how the project will affect the bottom line, not all that scientific stuff."

2. Briefings should be done by someone else.

   "I sit through these meetings, and it's uncomfortable for both of us. I just wait until it's over, then call the project manager or someone to answer my questions. It seems like a big waste of time for all."

PRESENTER'S NOTES

First of all, we looked through e-mail and phone logs of customer comments and complaints.

Both of these comments really show how the content of these briefings is not hitting the mark. The second comment is very interesting. This particular customer goes to expertise outside of engineering for clarification.

It is time to rethink the goals for the briefings. If they are, as was stated at the start, to inform customers about our work and to generate positive feelings about the engineering function, *it isn't happening.*

EXHIBIT 8.4. BRIEFING ABOUT THE ENGINEERING BRIEFINGS, *continued.*

Engineers Don't Like Briefings

- There is insufficient time for planning and delivering briefings ("not their real job").

- Customers don't seem to appreciate briefings.

- Briefings are not valued by the organization.
  - Supervisors would prefer that we not do briefings.
  - There are no rewards or incentives for those who do briefings.
  - Briefings sometimes result in negative consequences such as a backlog of "more important" project work.

PRESENTER'S NOTES

Next, we interviewed two different groups of engineers. The interviews were informal, and we used open-ended questions to get the engineers to open up and express their attitudes. We talked to eight engineers in all.

1. Bullet two is in line with the customer comments. I can see how the engineers get this feeling.

2. Bullet three is most revealing. What do you make of these comments? Why would supervisors not want their engineers to do these briefings? Look at the comment here about "more important" work. Do supervisors and engineers know how important these briefings are to improving customer relationships? Do they believe it? I know this might be far-fetched, but are the briefings really that important to the clients? We may want to investigate further and see what customers think.

Supervisors Think Engineers Could Do Better

- Engineers don't care about doing briefings.
- Engineers could do better if they had the skills.
  - Engineers are ill prepared for briefings—no time for it.
  - Engineers don't know how to field customer questions using lay terms.
- There is not enough time for briefings.
  - Engineers get behind schedule when they do these briefings.
  - We don't like to pull them away from their *real* work.

PRESENTER'S NOTES

We also interviewed three managers. Two were supervisors to some of the engineers we interviewed, and one was from another department. Again, we used open-ended questions to flesh out their attitudes.

1. Why do you think that engineers don't care?

2. Bullet two is in line with some of the customer comments. Basically, the briefings aren't conveying what the customer wants to know.

3. Notice bullet three. This tells us that supervisors may not see the briefings as a priority. This seems to be similar to some comments made by the engineers. Also, is there a shortage of staff that causes a crunch when engineers are called away to do these briefings?

EXHIBIT 8.4. BRIEFING ABOUT THE ENGINEERING BRIEFINGS, *continued.*

Survey of Engineers

Survey items—based on comments from prior interviews

- List of eleven factors that could be "causing" poor briefings; participants asked to rate each
- Open-ended request for suggestions to improve briefings

E-mailed to 200 engineers

150 returned surveys

PRESENTER'S NOTES

Finally, we sent out a simple, two–item survey via e-mail to 200 engineers. You all have a copy of the survey in your briefing report.

The first item, to which 150 responded, asked, "Why do you think the briefings are not appreciated by customers?" The open-ended question yielded 60 responses.

We sent another e-mail to all the engineers with a summary of the results.

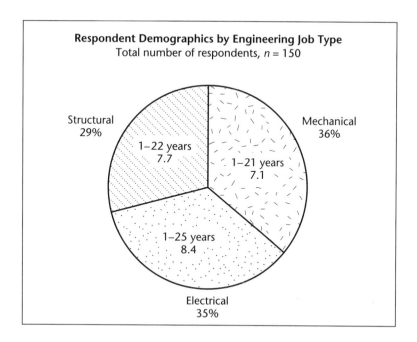

Respondent Demographics by Engineering Job Type
Total number of respondents, $n = 150$

Structural
29%

1–22 years
7.7

Mechanical
36%

1–21 years
7.1

1–25 years
8.4

Electrical
35%

PRESENTER'S NOTES

Here is a breakdown of survey respondents by their department. Notice that most respondents are mechanical engineers, but on average, the electrical engineers have been with the company longer.

We cross-tabulated the job type of the engineers with how they rated each factor. We found that for the top factors, neither longevity in the organization nor type of engineer made a difference.

EXHIBIT 8.4. BRIEFING ABOUT THE ENGINEERING BRIEFINGS, *continued.*

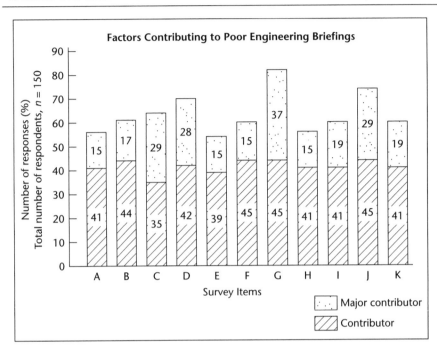

PRESENTER'S NOTES

Items were rated 0, not a contributing factor; 1, a factor; or 2, a major factor. As you can see, all items were seen as contributing to poor briefings by at least half of the respondents. Item E was the lowest-rated factor, with 54 percent rating it as a contributor. Item G was the highest rated, with 82 percent rating it as a factor.

Survey Items:
  A. Engineers aren't given sufficient time to plan the briefings.
  B. Engineers don't care about doing the briefings.
  C. Engineers don't know how to do briefings and speeches.
  D. Engineers are pulled away from their real work by the briefings.
  E. Engineers aren't good at those kinds of activities.
  F. Engineering supervisors don't encourage the briefings.
  G. Giving a good briefing doesn't count for anything.
  H. The people who give the good briefings aren't usually the best engineers.
  I. Engineers don't know how to plan the briefings.
  J. Engineers are the wrong people to do the briefings.
  K. Customers are the ones with the problem. They don't get technical content.

Chief Problem Areas

- Giving a good briefing doesn't count for anything (82 percent).

- Engineers are the wrong people to do the briefings (74 percent).

- Engineers are pulled away from their real work by the briefings (70 percent).

- Engineers don't know how to do briefings and speeches (64 percent).

PRESENTER'S NOTES

Here are the top four factors that engineers saw contributing to poor engineering briefings.

- Bullets one and three look to be related. It looks like the briefings aren't valued for some reason.

- Bullet two suggests we might have the wrong people doing the briefs. Who do you suppose would be the right people?

- Bullet four shows that the engineers realize they aren't hitting the target with customers. I bet this is really demotivating to these engineers, who are used to being experts at what they do.

EXHIBIT 8.4. BRIEFING ABOUT THE ENGINEERING BRIEFINGS, *continued.*

#1
A Good Briefing Doesn't Count for Much

15 percent suggested instituting proper incentives for engineers who do briefings.

"No one seems to appreciate that we do these briefings. It just seems like more work with no reward. In fact, we get just the opposite—more pressure because we get behind in our work when we have to do these briefings." [an experienced engineer]

PRESENTER'S NOTES

Sixty engineers chose to respond to question two in [the survey], answering an open-ended question suggesting how to improve engineering briefings. You'll notice that in all of the next few slides, these suggested solutions are consistent with the eleven-item question.

This particular comment illustrates the third most common suggestion given by engineers. It is in line with the number one rated item. Doesn't this sound like perhaps the briefings aren't being given a high enough priority in the organization? Or this priority isn't being communicated throughout the organization?

#2
Engineers Shouldn't Be the Ones
to Do the Briefings

47 percent suggested that someone besides engineers should
do the briefings.

"Engineers aren't good sales people. We're good at what
we do—let us do it! Leave the briefings to those who
have been trained to have people skills, like the project
managers." [mechanical engineer]

PRESENTER'S NOTES

This was the most common suggestion given by engineers. Once again, this comment supports the fact that these briefings don't have the proper focus in the engineering organization. Do they belong within that organization or elsewhere?

If the goals are information for customers and goodwill for engineering efforts, are there other ways to accomplish them?

EXHIBIT 8.4. BRIEFING ABOUT THE ENGINEERING BRIEFINGS, *continued.*

#3
Engineers Don't Know How to Do Briefings

32 percent expressed the need for better tools or support for engineers who do briefings.

"The customers don't seem to like our presentations. Either they don't care, or we're over their heads—too technical. We could use some sort of template or list of important points that the customers are really interested in knowing before we get out there."

PRESENTER'S NOTES

This was the second most common suggestion given by engineers. This is interesting. Notice where it says that "the customers don't seem to like our presentations." Based on this, the engineers think they don't know how to do briefings. Could it be that they just haven't been informed of the essential customer needs? Wouldn't it be great to find out from customers what they really want?

Any comments? I know that some of these findings are a little different from what you expected.

Questions for SemiCon to Consider

Why do we do briefings? Do we still consider them an important part of our strategy?

Are our assumptions about the value of briefings accurate? Do they enhance customer relations and education? How could that goal be more effectively accomplished?

What is an excellent client briefing? What does the client wish to gain?

Are we willing to do what must be done?

PRESENTER'S NOTES

Here are some issues we think might warrant further investigation and discussion. Any others you want to add?

EXHIBIT 8.4. BRIEFING ABOUT THE ENGINEERING BRIEFINGS, *continued.*

Next Steps: Focus on Strategy and Customers

Where to from here?

- Solicitation of opinions and questions from customers
- Strategic planning for engineering leadership to revisit basic purposes and possibilities
- Reconsider the job of the engineers. Are they the best people to do the briefings?

```
┌─────────────────────────────────────────────────────────┐
│                    Time Line                            │
│                                                         │
│     Phase one:          April 1 through May 5           │
│                                                         │
│     Customers:          May 8 through May 19            │
│                                                         │
│     Strategic planning:  May 22 through June 16         │
│                                                         │
│     Final meeting:       Between June 19 and July 5     │
│                                                         │
│                                                         │
│                                                         │
│                                                         │
│                                                         │
└─────────────────────────────────────────────────────────┘
```

PRESENTER'S NOTES

We've completed phase one. Phase two will involve constructing interviews and conducting them with customers.

Our final effort will be to conduct meetings with managers and the executive council to revisit some hard questions about the needs of customers, which we're going to examine in the next phase of this effort, and about alternative ways that the company might attempt to address these needs.

◆ ◆ ◆

There are some principles that drive effective reporting:

- Report throughout the effort, thereby avoiding surprises. Most customers don't like them. Involve customers in the effort, as that will increase both their comfort with the results of the performance analysis and the likelihood that they'll do something with them.
- Construct messages that are targeted to the customer and his realities; you may need to build model presentations or reports that will help him communicate to his leaders.
- Consider three approaches to making recommendations: the first is to make the recommendations and provide data-driven support for your perspectives; the second is to share the data and ask the customer what she perceives to be the implications; the third is to combine the first two approaches.
- Consider a two-pronged reporting strategy that involves both print and presentations. Some clients like one; some, the other; and some will require both.
- Think ahead to what the customer might want to do with the data. You might build a sample briefing for her to use in reporting back to the troops or executives, drafts of descriptions for new classes or policies that might result, and even sample newsletter copy. Show that you're concerned with how the customer will take the effort and make it useful.

CHAPTER NINE

TALES FROM THE TRENCHES

Allison: I've enjoyed reading your stories. The tales are great, meaty, sometimes funny. Did they really happen?

Kendra: I bet you could find the same two situations I describe in just about any school district in America. It was interesting to think about the problems and successes that are established up front, during planning.

Terry: Nothing fishy about my story. It happened to me. It describes some organizational realities and a mistake I made in positioning my analysis and in involving executives.

Fernanda: I talked about my experiences with analysis in three countries. It's how I saw it and still see it. When you work in a consulting company, the relationship between sales and performance analysis is inextricable.

Susan: My story happened to me at the beginning of my career, while I was in graduate school, but it still rings true. Orientation is the most prevalent form of "training." It's everywhere. Not exactly exotic. You'd think it would be simple to define a system. It wasn't. We really needed to do analysis.

Jeremy: What happened to me was pretty recent, not long before I joined Oracle. And I think you will find yourselves engaged in the kind of project I took on. Mine was about new technologies for training and knowledge management.

In this chapter, five professionals tell stories about how they responded to challenges, problems, and opportunities in their organizations: first is Kendra Sheldon, with a tale about technology innovation in public education; second, Terry Bickham, who describes a program to help Coast Guard people enforce complicated government regulations regarding fish and fishing; third is Fernanda Gimenez, who takes us to three countries, for short tales about consulting organizations doing performance analysis for their clients; fourth is Susan Olsen-Madeira, with a tale about the study she and an associate did to develop an orientation program for a large franchise company; and fifth, Jeremy Barnett takes us into the future with an analysis to prepare an organization to use emergent technologies to enhance sales performance.

Technology Innovation in Schools

While Kendra Sheldon is completing her master's at San Diego State University, she's been working on a technology innovation project funded by Pacific Bell. Her work involves her in districts, schools, and classrooms across California. Kendra's two tales show us the opposite sides of a coin in public education. It isn't only Vice President Gore who is enthusiastic about what technology can mean in schools and classrooms.

Who Wouldn't Want Computers in Their Classroom? Kendra Sheldon's Story

The cry "A computer in every classroom!" can be heard across the land like a mantra. Cookie sales, car washes, and bingo nights are epidemic as schools zealously raise money for technology. Parents, starry-eyed with dreams of computer-literate, Internet-savvy children, reach deep into their pockets to support their dreams. Educators, under pressure to prepare students for the twenty-first-century workplace, lend their support. Classrooms without computers are becoming the exception—not the rule.

This massive technology rollout has created a tremendous need for professional development, as educators are expected not only to use the technology but also to crank out computer-literate students. If ever there was a need for analysis before action, this is it, and considering that school officials value education and training more than most professionals, making the case for performance analysis should be a piece of cake, right?

Case One: Rancho Bizarro Elementary School

In Northern California, the strong economy has fueled a growth spurt in once-sleepy suburbs; new homes are sold months before they are built. Competition for home buyers is fierce. In one affluent suburb, Mr. McBuild, a large construction company, decides that the way to buyers' hearts is not with brass bathroom fixtures or bonus rooms but with a brand-new, high-tech elementary school. After all, what parent can resist the dream of computer-literate children taking their rightful places in Silicon Valley?

Mr. McBuild's new homes sell like hotcakes as the airwaves are flooded with ads: "Nothing is more important than your child's education. Rancho Bizarro Elementary, with computers in every classroom, e-mail and Internet access for all, will prepare your child for the twenty-first century. Why settle for anything less? Buy a Mr. McBuild home today . . . for your child's future." Rancho Bizarro Elementary is a success story . . . or is it?

As time goes on, parents begin to complain that their children are not developing computer skills, only better CD-ROM game strategies. Students gradually lose interest in technology as they come to see computers as second-rate Nintendo sets. Teachers endure countless mind-numbing sermons on the power of technology but fail to develop the most basic computer skills. Most use the computer as a typewriter. Support for Rancho Bizarro wanes as the community wonders what went wrong.

For Rancho Bizarro and other schools, the morning after has come. Administrators, teachers, and librarians are asking themselves, "Now that we have it, how will we use it?" They're realizing that computer use is anything but intuitive; many educators have never used one, let alone taught others how. It seems that as the PTA busily calculated how much technology they could purchase, nobody thought to train the teachers to plan to use it well.

Rancho Bizarro's problems might have been avoided if school officials had invested in performance analysis. If they had, they would have discovered that teachers need hands-on technology training, not lectures; they need job aids, not technical manuals; and they need long-term coaching and support, not a "one-day dip." A few interviews would have shed light on Rancho Bizarro's problems—and matched solutions to those problems:

The administrators say, "They've already had three in-services; why can't they use it?"

The parents say, "Teachers have tons of free time. If they need training, let them do it on their own time, not my child's."

The teachers say, "I don't want e-mail or the Internet; my students will just use it to download pornography."

Rancho Bizarro's situation is not unique. The problems come, in large part, from leaping without planning. The next case study shows that performance analysis can go a long way toward improving technology integration in the schools.

Case Two: Turtle Middle School

The Information Age has been a boon to small and midsize cities throughout the nation, as many high-tech companies have chosen clean air, hills of green, and ten-minute commutes over big-city woes. Affluent employees have happily relocated, taking their tax dollars with them.

Turtle Middle School, built during the prosperous Eisenhower years, has enjoyed a solid academic reputation for decades, despite its location in a poor, big-city neighborhood. Many proud staff members have been at Turtle since the very first day. Though money is scarce, the school has put together a technology program, one "hand-me-down" computer at a time. When the school reached the milestone "computer in every classroom," officials decided that it was time to launch an official technology program.

When a Plan Is Not a Plan Turtle Middle School was determined to make its technology program a success, and they hired media specialist Tiffany Banana to head up the effort. The first order of business was to write a technology plan to prepare the school for the twenty-first century. Tiffany's plan—a high-tech wish list of computer hardware, software, and speedy phone lines—was eagerly endorsed by city officials, school administrators, parents, and local businesses, who showed their support with more dona-tions. Turtle's teachers watched in stunned silence as their school was rapidly transformed into a "wired learning community."

Tiffany became well known to the faculty as she set up computing sta-tions in every classroom and gave every teacher a pile of how-to manu-als. Turtle's technology program appeared to be off to a running start—or was it?

An Ounce of Insight Is Worth a Pound of Technology As Tiffany traveled from classroom to classroom, installing "new-better-faster" software, she noticed two things: the teachers did not seem to be using their com-puters, and they seemed to resent her more than a little bit. Tiffany decided to call her friend Jack Bright, a performance specialist, and ask for his advice.

Tiffany: Jack, I don't know what to do. I've given these teachers the latest software, hardware, and documentation, but they are just not using them. Worse yet, they seem to resent me. What am I doing wrong?

Jack: Tiffany, did anyone ever think to ask the teachers how they felt about the new technology program? Technology is great, but the teachers are the ones who have to use it. Maybe you should talk to them to find out what's going on. Also, what are their skills? Are they novices or experts? Spend a day asking questions, and you'll know what's going on and what you might try next.

Tiffany: OK, I'll give it a try. But what do feelings have to do with computers? Everyone was so excited about my technology program; you'd think the teachers would plunge into those manuals so they could get on-line.

Analysis Turns Things Around Tiffany took Jack's advice and spoke to several teachers about the new technology program. She asked the following questions:

How do you feel about the new technology program?

Tell me a little about your computer skills.

What would you like to use the computers to do?

What questions do you want answered about computers in your classroom?

Are you interested in hands-on training to develop computer skills?

In what other ways might I support your efforts?

Tiffany also perused the manuals and spent some time using the new hardware and software herself.

A Data-Driven Solution System Tiffany found a widespread lack of enthusiasm, even resentment toward the technology initiative. She also discovered that the how-to manuals were less than helpful and that using the new software was not intuitive. Tiffany also found herself struggling to understand the on-line help systems. Soon she came to understand the teachers' feelings about her and the great new opportunity.

Tiffany's findings are typical of new system rollouts that overlook the people side of things. Fortunately, the data she gleaned from analysis helped her design a customized solution system to make Turtle Middle School's technology program a success. It emphasizes the uses teachers most value and relies on a familiar instructor, available coaching, and simplified job aids. School officials and faculty, motivated to maintain Turtle's reputation for excellence, supported these recommendations, and the program is starting to become a high-tech success story.

Serving a Government Mandate

Terry Bickham now directs the U.S. Coast Guard's training center in Petaluma, California. This is a story about an attempt to respond to a problem the agency was having with enforcing fishing regulations. The analysis is certainly interesting, but most intriguing is how difficult it was to put the solution system in place.

Fish Things First: Terry Bickham's Story

A few years ago, a government study confirmed the commercial fishing industry's view that Coast Guard officers who enforced living marine resource laws weren't up to speed on fish, fishermen, or the process of catching fish. Admittedly, being a fish cop was not viewed by most as on par with the more glamorous missions of saving lives and catching drug smugglers. Proficiency at it was not a priority.

To right the situation, Congress promptly legislated money to buy a training fix. Being largely responsible for performance improvement in the Pacific region, I got a call from headquarters in Washington, D.C., letting me know that additional staff and funding were on the way to help me put together a training program for the Coast Guard folks on the West Coast. I was expected to start formal classes on fisheries law enforcement in about two months.

I had a lot of questions that weren't getting answers. What *really* was the problem? What were we doing in that arena that was not so good or good enough? How could technology help? What exactly was headquarters attempting to achieve? This situation was ripe for performance analysis.

First Step

Soon, half a dozen new employees and a meager budget augmentation showed up on my office doorstep, all assigned to the fish challenge. What wasn't surprising was that these prospective "trainers" had neither fish nor instructional design expertise. The clock was ticking, so I promptly gave these folks a speedy indoctrination in performance analysis and divided them into three teams. One team would concentrate on the Pacific Northwest, one on California, and the last on the western Pacific islands. Each team would focus on gathering data from their respective geographic regions. Chunking it up helped make sense of the challenge. I left the teams to gather and review the literature on fisheries in their regions, records of inspections, court case packages, trade journals, and so on, while I pressed headquarters about expectations.

The fisheries enforcement office at headquarters didn't have the details I needed regarding optimals. Basically, they expected a formal regional fisheries training center to be established. Their vision focused on facilities and curriculum. The best I could determine, they wanted something like a week-long Fisheries Enforcement 101 course, and they wanted it fast. Reading the government study was slightly more enlightening. Although it lacked specific information about the Pacific region, it did point out that fisheries training to date was informal and inadequate. The reference section was a great source of professional writings on the subject.

After a couple of days of heavy-duty Web surfing and good old library research, we found out that fisheries in the Pacific region were dissimilar. Salmon trolling off Washington state and tuna seining in the South Pacific were as different as baking and grilling. Sea urchin diving off of southern California was one example of a myriad of small regional fisheries. Each fishery had its own set of complex and volatile laws and regulations.

Environmentalists and the fishing industry were at odds over species catch limits. All agreed that the fish were disappearing, and blamed each other. The outcome of this effort was that my teams had quickly amassed a good foundation on what types of fishing were going on in their regions and who the players were.

Next Steps

I sat down with the teams to sketch out the next several stages of our analysis. We set up a series of interviews for the following week with various sources in each geographic region. The teams would first go to the respective regional Coast Guard law enforcement manager (both a customer and a local sponsor) to get his or her view of the problem. Each team would then spend a couple of days out in the field interviewing Coast Guard officers who were expected to do fish inspections (the job incumbents) and their immediate supervisors. Next, the teams would visit with state and federal game wardens (experts) and fishermen (experts, customers). We developed a structured interview job aid with questions for each source tailored to gathering facts and feelings about what was and should be happening.

What We Found

By the end of that week, we had an enormous amount of data. As expected, regional managers perceived training and enforcement efforts as inadequate. We learned that most Coast Guard officers shied away from enforcing fisheries laws because the regulations were too complex, all the fish looked the same, and the officers really felt uncomfortable trying to enforce something they admittedly knew little about. Besides, it was a smelly, thankless task that competed with their primary job of rescuing people. Though most felt professionalism required a reasonable proficiency, the prospect of spending a week out of town in a class about fish law was not at all attractive.

Fishers, the preferred nongender-specific term for fishermen, were riled that officers who knew virtually nothing about what they were doing were coming on their boats to inspect them. Short-staffed state and federal game wardens required experienced Coast Guard officers to help them out but lamented that there was little communication between them. For example, at one Coast Guard station, the Coasties complained they didn't know what the current fisheries laws were in their area and hadn't a clue how to find out. When I pointed out that a federal fisheries enforcement office was located in the building next door, it was news to them.

After investing about a week in the performance analysis, it was obvious that a forty-hour resident course couldn't cure these ills. The situation differed as you moved fifty miles up or down the coast. Sure, training would be a key part of the solution, and I planned a full-blown training needs assessment to yield the meat for subsequent lesson plans and job aids. Right up front, though, the performance analysis showed the need for a solution system that established partnerships among the players to share information and eliminate barriers.

What Happened

Here's what we did. Knowledgeable state and federal officers mentored Coast Guard folks in fisheries enforcement and conducted joint enforcement patrols with them. A greater sense of professionalism emerged. Changes in regulations were shared via newly set up e-mail and fax networks to demystify the law. State and federal fisheries biologists frequently visited Coast Guard stations with fresh-caught fish and provided clues on how to identify them. These scientists also shared data to show the status of depleted fish stocks and discussed the positive impact enforcement efforts were having on the health of species. The Coast Guard officers learned firsthand that they played an important part in living marine resource protection and contributed to the economic viability of their communities.

Coast Guard officers established relationships and a dialogue with local fishers and fishing organizations. Regular discussion groups were organized as a forum to clear up misunderstandings and balance enforcement with a sense of fairness. Fishers shared how being stopped for an inspection impacted their bottom line. Some of them invited local Coasties onto their boats and explained to them how the gear worked. A few even volunteered their boats as platforms for practice inspections. Coasties visited local wholesale fish auctions and net storage barns to further their knowledge about the industry.

Once the performance analysis was complete, my trainers continued to expand their expertise and develop specific one- or two-day training for each region and, in many cases, specialized modules appropriate to stretches of coastline in each region. Instead of a resident course, the trainers delivered their classes on-site at the local stations and spent time there to ensure relevance. These classes were hands-on and tailored to the locale, and involved community fishers. Demand for the classes was high, and the trainers were welcomed as part of the crew.

After a while, Coast Guard expertise and participation in fisheries enforcement increased, and complaints from fishers dwindled. Everyone seemed happier. Well, not everyone.

Some in Washington were still expecting us to produce that training center. They had pictured bricks and mortar, and I hadn't given it to them. Of course, what we did on the West Coast went beyond just putting on a class. It was a successful systemic solution costing one-tenth what a comparable training center would have. Where did I go wrong? I had missed the boat by not adequately sharing the results of the performance analysis or selling our solution system to headquarters as we moved forward with it. I had concentrated on fixing the problem without bringing the sponsor along. It's been three years, and we haven't gotten their full backing yet. Not yet.

Performance Analysis Here, There, and Everywhere

Fernanda Gimenez now lives and works in the Netherlands. Now a human performance consultant for Origin Corporation, she goes back a few years to describe analysis experiences in the United States and Argentina. Fernanda describes the sobering effects of business realities on the front end. It should come as no surprise that speed and customer delight rule.

Conducting Analysis in Three Different Worlds: Fernanda Gimenez's Story

Multinational Consulting Firm: U.S. Experience

The first year and a half of my career, I worked at the San Diego branch of a large multinational consulting firm. I soon learned that all the analysis methodology I had read was not exactly aligned with practice. I had read that the analysis phase was important and critical; however, it rarely happened because our budget was scarce, and the costs were not easily recovered afterwards.

The goal of our analysis was to sell our products and to create a high-level work plan (including time and budget). Speed was a key performance indicator for this analysis. The strategy consisted of one or two of our highly experienced professionals interviewing key available personnel. ("Available" was a stronger criterion than "key.") We believed more experienced professionals could guess and guess-estimate quicker and more accurately than the typical worker.

When we got to the conclusions of the projects, we blamed budget overruns on overlooked factors such as the culture of the organization and the authority, knowledge level, and availability of the people. I can't remember that the overruns were ever blamed on the lack of accurate analysis information.

As I look back, I can say that the front-end analysis played a great role *in theory*, but in practice, it didn't really happen. It was part of the selling process, performed before the formal proposal was written.

Multinational Consulting Firm: Buenos Aires

When I moved to the Third World, I became an expert. (This promotion took place as the airplane crossed the equator—I was asleep at the time.) All of a sudden, I was a source of information, a literature adviser, and a tool builder so that all those without the expertise could run analysis and implement the appropriate training and performance support solutions ("appropriate" meaning within budget, given the consultants and client resources available). It was a real test of my skills as a human performance technologist.

Analysis was brief, very brief. It was usually run after a technology manager had promised the client to train the whole workforce in half a day. Regardless of the difficult situation set for the analysis, we managed to run it very fast and somewhat effectively.

I created a basic list of questions to gather audience, goal, and task information for each intervention, based on our own methodology and standards, my limited experience, and a book I'd read called *Training*

Needs Assessment. I was a backup and supervisor for all analyses, and often was the intervention designer. Luckily, almost all projects were related to technology implementation.

Sometimes we were fortunate, and the personnel department possessed current workforce information (age, experience, position, education level) and was willing to share it with us. Then we didn't have to go out and gather information anew. I would say this happened half the time. The other, less fortunate half, we scanned the workplace and asked managers or employees (or both) about themselves and their associates. Most of the time, workers knew a lot about each other, and they gave us a general picture of the population.

Our task analysis was based on the documentation of the technology system. To gather an idea of the way the system would be changing, we compared the new one with existing documents regarding the previous system. Meanwhile, the rest of the project team and the client wondered why we were asking so many irrelevant questions and wasting precious time while they worked their tails off in serious activities.

Our goal was to justify why we could not train the whole workforce in half a day, as promised earlier by the project manager. Then, based on the results of our brief analysis, we created a quick-and-dirty proposal for the project owners. This proposal presented a training and performance support intervention that would *actually* enable the workforce to use the new technology once it was on-line. Fortunately, most Argentine managers were very reasonable and enlarged the training and support budget to match our proposal. Once we convinced our managers, and they convinced the client, we started to work.

We created information interventions based on what we found during the front end. We had templates to which we adapted the existing system information. In the first projects, we found poorly written documents, without standards, which took a long time to transform into real information that the users—or anyone in their right mind—could understand. Later, we created templates for system designers and programmers to document system functionality. These workers are effective at applying standards. In later projects, as we got better at providing templates for them to fill in, we generated system documents that were assembled into electronic performance support systems (EPSS) almost without modifications.

Creating training was a bit more complicated. We had templates, but we required business information to set realistic scenarios in which using the system made sense. This required time from the users involved in the project, who were for the most part overworked with system revisions and testing. We who had been perceived as wasting time at the start were now asking for their help, a situation that sometimes strained relationships yet usually led to better programs.

In summary, the analysis phase was a sketchy procedure run in order to get the budget and time allocation to create effective interventions. It was not recognized as a formal project phase, although it played a key role in the official documented methodology sold by the consulting firm, and, in practice, it had a dramatic impact on the overall project.

Yet Another Multinational Consulting Firm: Holland

At age twenty-eight, I followed my heart and relocated in Holland. I continue to work in the field, but now in a setting that favors projects for European multinational clients. This provides for additional language and cultural flavors. Here, we run the analysis phase under a short-term, separate contract. This phase varies in length and depth according to the number and diversity of client sites and the agreement with the client. During this analysis, we determine the costs, time line, and strategy for the whole project and create a high-level project plan and proposal.

Considering the cultural and language differences, we usually have a core team (specialized in training and performance support) that coordinates, guides, and supports local teams. There is a set of standard tools and templates that facilitates the coordination and execution of this phase.

Amazingly, here in Holland we are congruent in theory and in practice. We view this phase as a stand-alone project with its own commercial agreement, budget, and time line, for the purpose of setting a clear framework for the work to come. I must say that my experience in Holland is at this point very limited, and time will show me whether things will turn out as good as they look at this early point. For the time being, I am enjoying my romance.

A Fresh Look at Orientation

Susan Olsen-Madeira, now a lead product manager at Microsoft, reaches into her graduate student past to present a tale that still rings true. Here we see external consultants grapple with strategies to shift their customer from one view of what ought to be done to another. An additional wrinkle: the analysis unearthed a front-and-center role for line managers. What are you going to do when the managers are reluctant?

Orientation: Susan Olsen-Madeira's Story

A franchising company's headquarters had for several years experienced increases in the number of employees. What was once a small business environment—where each knew the other—had become a large, impersonal corporate headquarters. This increased number of employees along with a rising turnover rate ensured a pool of "new employees" at the headquarters. The new employees were expected to understand the corporate organization and learn new culture, computer, phone, and other systems. Employees were also expected to know how corporate served the franchise offices throughout the world.

Prior to these years of growth, headquarters had grown slowly; there was not a strong need or desire for a formalized employee orientation program. As each new employee was hired, he or she was treated to a personalized orientation and introductions. However, as the number of new employees climbed, Ted Bryant, the director of human resources, realized that it was time to implement a formal orientation program. He had a pretty good idea about how the program ought to work.

Initial Plan

To implement his program, Ted turned to Cora Clay, the training director, for assistance in developing his orientation program. Ted felt the program should consist of four half-day sessions that included informational workshops and departmental tours, along with a hiring manager's checklist that would assist managers in orienting their new employees.

Due to resource constraints, Cora decided to hire two instructional design consultants, Leah and me, to develop Ted's orientation program. Leah and I had reservations about Ted's approach to orientation. Although orientation programs are nothing new, and most companies have very similar programs, we felt the need to perform further analysis before starting development.

Process

We approached senior and middle management and employees for insight into their needs and concerns associated with the orientation process. We used interviews, questionnaires, and a focus group to investigate and document the needs. We also scanned the published literature. The following paragraphs outline the data-collection process we used during the analysis.

Interviews. We began the data-collection process by conducting twelve interviews. Six of the interviews were with employees who had been with the company for less than six months. The other six were with those who had been with the company for at least one year. We asked the new employees to voice their orientation needs and to share the frustrations and problems they were experiencing. We asked the long-term employees what they felt would have helped them become better oriented to the company. Both groups provided information and resources that would benefit new hires. We also interviewed the CEO of the franchise company. His personality and presence set the tone for the organization, a spirit that should be reflected in the orientation program.

Questionnaire. We distributed a questionnaire to all employees at the headquarters. The questionnaire asked employees to identify their most important orientation topics, the biggest problems for new employees, and what they felt managers should do to orient new employees.

Focus Group. We summarized the findings gathered from these strategies and presented them to a nine-member focus group consisting of directors, managers, and a vice president. The goals of this group were to

- Report findings to management
- Discuss management's role in the orientation process
- Generate ideas, concerns, and constraints in regards to the orientation process
- Determine necessary resources to assist management in their new orientation roles, if any

Obstacles

The process to define and rejuvenate this orientation was not remarkable. Worth noting, however, are the obstacles we faced during and after the analysis.

For example, when Ted met with us, he told us what the orientation program would be; Ted's expectations were that we would immediately begin development of the program as he defined it.

With Cora's help, we explained to Ted the importance of taking a fresh look at the situation, of involving not only members of the human resources organization but also employees from all levels and organizations at headquarters, prior to defining the program. Getting Ted's support was not difficult. Ted had complete confidence in Cora, and Cora knew we were employing sound instructional design principles. As the project progressed, we sent frequent meeting minutes and other necessary correspondence. Throughout the process, we kept Ted informed about our activities and about how these efforts fit into the development of the orientation.

Time was another obstacle. Upper management wanted the orientation program delivered in less than two months. There were two obvious reasons for this push. First, at the previous corporate meeting attended by all employees, the suggestion for an orientation had been made and had received great response. Several months had passed since this meeting, and the leadership did not wish to dawdle in its response.

Second, the corporate mission and vision statements had recently been revised. The new statements included words like "team" and "quality," and the executive management team felt a orientation program for new employees would be a good place to start to make these statements come to life.

The reasons for the rush were certainly valid, but the time was insufficient for designing and developing the orientation program given the available resources. In order to deal with the constraints, we analyzed the reasons for the push. We determined that taking visible steps toward an orientation program and building enthusiasm for the development of the program would handle the concerns of upper management, even if the orientation program wasn't completed in two months. This time constraint was one of the reasons that we sent all employees questionnaires. It was critical that everyone saw some progress and felt a sense of ownership. This philosophy was congruent with the new corporate mission and vision.

The final obstacle was the political nature of the project. There were several issues, but two were particularly interesting. First, although managers' involvement and the ensuring of consistency were common themes throughout the interview and questionnaire responses, several managers saw an orientation program as one change they didn't need. Some seemed to fight the responsibility of orienting their new employees. This situation could not be ignored if the final orientation program was to be successful.

The second issue was that study had uncovered numerous requests for written job descriptions. Written job descriptions were not a standard practice, and Ted and Cora warned us about raising the issue to the executive management team. We felt we had to address the issue of job descriptions, but we had to do it without offending the management team or the people who had hired us.

The management focus group, besides fulfilling the objectives outlined earlier, was a means for addressing these political issues. We directed the discussion and presented results in such a way that the focus-group members themselves raised the subjects of management involvement and job descriptions. Thus the members of the focus group did not become defensive about these issues and willingly discussed them.

Results

From this performance analysis, we developed a plan for a major orientation program. The program contained some of Ted's original requests but differed in many respects, particularly pointing toward a larger and defined role for managers, a self-orientation for new employees, a video to provide a consistent message, print materials to which new employees could refer, and structured department tours by managers.

Although the orientation program was an important intervention, we recommended several other interventions that could help all employees adjust to the changing corporate environment. These recommendations included the following:

- A library for manuals, a centralized location for all office system documentation, policy and procedure manuals, training manuals, guides, and the like. The library would contain one or two copies of the most up-to-date version of the documentation. Employees would always know where they could go to find a needed reference.
- A letter of acceptance (and welcoming) sent out to all new employees.
- A complete set of job descriptions.
- A human resources pool for those who want to develop career paths. When job openings occur, offices in other areas of the country would look to corporate's human resources pool prior to looking outside the company, and vice versa.
- A series of mini-seminars presented at corporate. Seminars would include the "ins and outs" of a particular department and overviews of the business, of new office systems, of the computer software, and so on. A schedule and guidelines for attending the seminars would be sent out to all employees.

Lessons Learned

Everyone involved with the analysis viewed it as a success, but all of us had thoughts about what we could have done differently, what we might not do again, and what we will use in future projects:

- Increase communication about the process ahead of time, clarifying roles and responsibilities.
- Propose the study by using key words or "hot buttons" that make the process hard to refuse. For example, a key word for management might be *productivity*. If the performance analysis is defined as "a means of determining what the new employee needs in order to be productive," or as "a means of determining the topics to be addressed so that orientation is both effective and efficient," it will sell the concept more readily.
- Be cautious in "choosing your battles." Cora believes strongly in analysis but tends to approach it a little differently now. Whereas in the past she would never design a program before completing some prior analysis, she now believes it is sometimes better not to fight the political battle up front. In certain situations, where timing is critical or there are political overtones affecting the process, Cora says she doesn't push for a strong analysis up front but instead does a very quick study, far less even than was done here, and a more substantive needs assessment or evaluation at the back end of a project, knowing revisions will be made.
- Keep good documentation; it is critical. Not only was documentation useful in keeping all team members (external and internal) informed, but it has a post-project purpose as well. Cora says that she still refers to information contained in the report. The documentation reminds her of changes that still need to take place as well as provides her a database and grounding point for future projects.
- Use focus groups. The focus group for this project, in which key decision makers were gathered to discuss the findings, concerns, and possible interventions, was and is a useful tool. It ensured buy-in and provided great insights!

Technology and the Future

Jeremy Barnett describes one of his projects as director of learning technologies at Knowledge Stream Partners in Los Angeles. He took on a challenge that parallels issues that many of us confront now or will be confronting soon. Jeremy was asked to help a large sales organization manage its shift to emergent technologies like CD-ROM and the Internet. The organization planned to do training using these technologies. Jeremy's study took him and the client in additional strategic directions.

Setting the Stage for On-Line Training and Performance Support: Jeremy Barnett's Story

On a recent engagement, I had the opportunity to consult with the sales organization of a large retailer. They hired our firm because they were planning significant growth for the coming year and needed to codify their approaches to training and development. There was also a need to extend the training out to multiple sites throughout the country, and they wanted to exploit the advantages of multimedia. They put the charge like this: "We need a training system. And we think it should be on our Intranet or maybe CD-ROM." Caught up in a large-scale initiative to leverage the Web as well as to support the corporate multimedia training strategy, they saw a great opportunity to set the pace for the organization.

Getting the Client Beyond Training

Our initial challenge was to help our clients think beyond traditional training problems and solutions. Although their focus was on "teaching people to do their jobs better," they didn't have a clear understanding of what that meant for new hires, veteran employees, and the different roles played within the departments.

Training means different things to different people; to this retailer it meant the antidote for product knowledge deficiencies, poor customer-interaction procedures, and inadequate sales performance. We were skeptical that a Web-based training system in and of itself would or could solve these complex and important challenges.

Although we knew that Web-based training alone wasn't sufficient, we also realized that *our* feelings and experience would not be sufficient to move our customers toward a more appropriate system. We needed data. We needed to better understand the actual performance issues according to managers, sales reps, and customer survey data. With better insight, we could then help our client distinguish the "learning" needs from the "performance support" needs and the solutions necessary to bridge the gaps.

To help make that distinction and identify the performance problems that were impacting their business, we recommended that, prior to developing courseware, we invest some time in conducting a performance analysis. They agreed to a snappy two-week analysis. Going through that analysis together helped define appropriate courseware and brought the client and Knowledge Stream together in a common vision for the project.

Performance Analysis Is a Critical Component of Performance-Centered Design

Nowhere is the distinction between training needs assessment and performance analysis manifested more clearly than in the design of performance support software. And moving our client from a training mind-set to a performance support approach was not easy. The performance analysis provided tangible activities and outcomes to which our client resonated:

• The performance analysis established the parameters of the system design and development effort. To set expectations, we gently reminded our client that no software is going to be the panacea for all organizational ills. Therefore, prior to development, it was important to establish what it is the system is going to accomplish and what problems it won't solve. The PA also focused our attention on the various factors or drivers that would contribute to these critical changes.

• The performance analysis provided the baseline measures for evaluating the program. To help our client assess the value of their investment in the project, we supported their effort in establishing the criteria for evaluation. The PA in the first stages of design helped to identify those measures that the system would address: an increase in the number of calls handled by service reps, reduced waiting time for customers, increased customer satisfaction scores, and so on.

We used performance analysis to uncover optimal and actual behavior as well as current drivers and matched solutions. First, we looked closely at the sales process. We identified the current workflow and an optimal customer-interaction sales model. We also sought insight into the daily work of the sales representatives. Finally, we catalogued and evaluated existing information and support resources.

In efforts to encourage our client to think beyond training problems to a more comprehensive approach, we asked them to hear from their own people about issues beyond the training curriculum. So we designed the interview questions to uncover managers' issues with overall staff productivity as well as sales reps' perspectives on the current computer system, the product information resources, the customer-interaction process, and the existing training resources.

To gain a broad perspective, we met with sales management, with outstanding sales and service representatives as well as average performers, and with new hires. Through group and individual interviews, we asked the participants about

• Typical work activities as well as uncommon but important activities
• What's working well and what isn't
• What matters most to customers and what impedes effective customer service
• The effectiveness of existing information systems (electronic as well as print material)
• The effectiveness of current training resources

The results of the interviews and workplace observations (as well as a cursory review of customer satisfaction surveys) yielded a performance analysis summary report. The report organized the feedback from the interviews into "needs during customer interactions" and "foundational knowledge needs." Based on this categorization, we could demonstrate the distinction between performance support resources (for use during customer interactions) and learning resources (to build foundational product and process knowledge). The table excerpts the results and recommendations.

The first column reflects the stages of the model workflow as identified by our sales process description. The second and third columns summarize the performance issues and existing resources. The fourth and fifth columns report recommended learning and performance support tools to be developed.

Sales Process Phase	Performance Issues	Current Resources	Recommended Learning Resources	Recommended Performance Support Resources
Access Customer Info	Computer systems: training is insufficient Phone coding is often incorrect	CBT and workbook	Web-based introduction to ten most common transaction screens Introduction to all tools	On-line index: "How Do I . . ." wizard
Greeting	None reported	New hire orientation and sales rep. guidebook	Web-based sales process tutorial: customer-interaction simulations Ghosting with checklist	Not applicable
Assess Customer Needs	Converting service or troubleshooting calls into sales opportunities Inefficient customer needs analysis Qualifying the caller is difficult	Product sheet (placemat job aid) Five-step interview approach On-line product reference	Sales process tutorial	"Investment needs assessor"—tool link into existing on-line product reference

Results of the Performance Analysis

Although the client was not yet prepared to move on all fronts, the performance analysis provided a menu of options and priorities and highlighted the key differences between training and performance support. We were now ready to share in the process of making informed decisions about how to structure the system, which modules to build first, and which problems should be addressed with Web-based tutorials rather than on-line tools to support customer interactions.

After the analysis, we rescoped the project with the strategy of developing three types of solutions, each of which would be supported by its own targeted training needs assessment.

1. Interactive tutorials to build foundational product knowledge for new hires
2. A Web-based product encyclopedia for real-time reference
3. A collection of performance support tools to enhance customer interactions

The PA also produced intangible results. By investing time to understand the company, we gained insight into its people, departments, and organization. A strong and trusting relationship between our organization and theirs resulted, and, most important, they came to agree to the mix of knowledge and training strategies. We didn't have to tell them. The PA process in which they participated did that for us.

Lessons Learned

The performance analysis yielded valuable insight for our clients, above and beyond their expectations about training. They appreciated the findings, and the PA triggered some new strategic planning for their career paths, employee development planning, product specialization, and the like.

If we had it to do over again, we would have established closer relationships with the company's internal organizational development and training department to ensure continued performance improvement.

◆ ◆ ◆

What are the lessons we can take away from these analysts' experiences? As adept as our storytellers were, none of these efforts was a slam dunk. Success involved planning the planning, bringing customers along slowly, and selling and marketing solutions that often differed from the customer's original scope and vision.

Selecting the right analysis tools for your purposes can be one of your most important analysis strategies. The data, and the collection methods, can provide you with direct and indirect benefits now and in the future. By using pointed questionnaire items that address underlying issues or by presenting delicate findings in a focus group of critical players, you can "let the data do the talking." This may get you off the hook as the bearer of bad news in touchy political situations or when buy-in is a major obstacle. Furthermore, the data you collect today could be used tomorrow to update materials or to justify a training needs assessment or the next phase of the project.

Different cultures vary widely in the way they value methods and solutions. Whether you are dealing with a culture in an organization or in a distant country, you will be faced with groups who either do or do not value front-end analysis. You must be able to communicate and market the process under varied circumstances, while maintaining a stance that brings your client along.

It is essential to get to the root cause behind any client request—not only to ensure an appropriate solution but also to select the right front-end approach. Why the time crunch? Why do they want the high visibility of a glossy course catalogue? By uncovering the real reasons behind the requests and carefully selecting your approach, you may relieve some of your client's immediate pressures and concerns, increasing receptivity to the solution you recommend.

Share the fun. Don't let them wonder what you're doing and why, and don't be satisfied with slipping your solution in through the back door. Involving your client in the analysis process can be the best way to sell your approach and solution system while fertilizing the environment for future client relations. Include all relevant stakeholders and a variety of sources. Share your results, provide options, and elicit input in the planning and prioritizing phases of the project to create a common vision.

CHAPTER TEN

INTO THE FUTURE

In this final chapter, I want to talk about some important influences on the field of human resources and training. My intention here is to provide a brief definition of these forces and what they mean to us as we plan. We'll focus on three trends: relationship management; knowledge management; and cognitive science. Technology, another major influence, was discussed in detail in Chapter Seven.

Relationship Management

In the past, many in our business have earned the title "order taker." Interactions often went like this:

> *Pro:* Glad you called. How can I help?
>
> *Customer:* Well, we're trying to cope with deregulation in the utilities industry here in California. Suddenly we're going to be tossed into a very competitive environment. I was thinking that you might come on out and do some stress management

>   workshops for us. Mindy—you know, the woman from
>   ASTD—said that you did a good one-day for her. That's
>   what we'd like for our supervisors too, although we'd prefer
>   the half-day class, if you have one. Our people are smart.
> *Pro:* Sure do have a half-day version. Happy to help out and glad
>   you called. When were you thinking about scheduling the ses-
>   sions? Let's get out our calendars.

An exaggeration? In some cases certainly, but there has been a tendency for human resources professionals to satisfy the request and to
jump to the solution, especially when it involves something they hold in
inventory. One justification for this behavior, congruent with the quality movement, is that it shows eagerness to delight our customers, at
least insofar as meeting their immediate, expressed needs.

A better way to approach the business is through relationship management—that is, through your long-term, deep, and constant relationship with the customer and with the customer's people, context, and
strategy. You aren't waiting to be asked to offer a class or to help with a
product rollout or to solve a problem with error rates or time management. You're aware already because you were in the room, at the table,
when opportunities and problems were bouncing about.

Sandy Quesada's global group at Eli Lilly Corporation is a good
example of internal relationship management. A lean central organization works closely with training and development professionals who
reside in the business units and in global regions. These professionals
are a part of the fabric of the pharmaceutical business, working side by
side with the researchers, sales and marketing professionals, manufacturers, information technologists, and others. Their primary perspective is that of the line unit and the geographic areas they serve,
recognizing that what China needs just now is different from what Australia and Germany need. Quesada's goal is to help them maintain that
focus, while encouraging them also to enjoy and develop the robust professional identity associated with our community of practice. Her team
does this by establishing common professional development opportunities, sharing best practices, and engaging in consultation across operat-

ing units. Although Quesada's entire effort is predicated on customer focus and collegiality, she has also established a central unit that specializes in performance consulting, headed by Janice Simmons.

Relationship management can apply to the external consultant as well. What characterizes it is the inclination to serve customer needs rather than to sell whatever it is the consultant holds in inventory. Customization dominates. Because the external consultant has prior knowledge of the situation and continuously "studies up" on the organization and related topics, he can exercise well-reasoned curiosity and skepticism. From time to time, anticipation becomes a real possibility, even for an external provider.

There is a growing body of literature nudging us toward this focus on customers, relationships, and tailored responses. The publication of *Performance Consulting* (Robinson & Robinson, 1995) brought this shift into the mainstream under the umbrella of performance consulting. Based on the work of Thomas Gilbert, Robert Mager, Peter Pipe, Joe Harless, Geary Rummler, Ron Zemke, and others, and on the impetus provided by the International Society for Performance Improvement, the Robinsons' book prodded internal trainers and human resources professionals and external consultants to rethink and expand their roles.

The new role of the performance consultant is predicated on analysis. If every interaction with clients and customers involves tailoring solutions to particular needs and circumstances, then analysis provides the defining energy and customer direction. As I said in my chapter in the *Handbook of Human Performance Technology* (Stolovitch, 1992), "Analysis provides the foundation for HPT, a profession and a perspective that demands study before recommendations, data before decisions, and involvement before actions."

Knowledge Management

The publication of Peter Senge's *The Fifth Discipline* in 1990, my coauthored *Handbook of Job Aids* in 1991, Thomas Stewart's *Intellectual Capital* in 1997, and Thomas Davenport and Lawrence Prusak's *Working Knowledge* in 1998 established knowledge management (KM) as a key focus for professionals concerned with human performance. Knowledge management directs attention to the information, both explicit and tacit, that resides in the organization and its people and to strategies for increasing the public presence, value, and accessibility of that information.

How do we capture the knowledge? How do we tease the subtle know-how and perspectives from, for example, a contracts administrator about strategies for maintaining productive and peaceful relationships with both the sales force *and* the legal staff? How do we help her describe the many things she considers and does, of which she isn't even aware? In addition, how do we ensure that a steady flow of explicit customer information is finding its way into databases so that, say, any salesperson visiting Costco is familiar with the terms of their most current contracts and formal and informal conversations. How do we find what it is that savvy sales people or responsive customer service reps or effective security personnel know? How do we make certain that the information reflects not just the obvious but also the more subtle and cultural aspects that are essential to success? How do we make it available to more people? How do we make it available in more ways? How do we begin to take advantage of technology to separate knowledge, expertise, and even wisdom from the people who tend to clutch it to their bosoms? How do we ensure that the information is refreshed? And how do we make certain that it is easily located at the moment of need?

If these questions are seriously entertained, a very different kind of organization and knowledge worker emerges. Thomas Stewart (1997, p. 111) quotes Charles Paulk of Andersen Consulting on knowledge management: "When one of our consultants shows up, the client should get the best of the firm, not just the best of the consultant." When a professional contributes to Paulk's goal, he or she is nurturing a learning organization. Such an entity treasures its intellectual capital, encourages sharing not hoarding, and values teams more than individual stars. Pursuing knowledge management in a learning organization stimulates additional questions about sources, such as the ones sprinkled throughout this handbook and presented in Table 10.1. The analyst turned knowledge manager is looking beyond the classroom or the individual

TABLE 10.1. TYPICAL QUESTIONS INFLUENCED BY KNOWLEDGE MANAGEMENT.

Aspects of KM	Analyst Queries
The organization actively collects the best thoughts, practices, and wisdom of its people and its customers.	How are we collecting examples of best practices, data on customers, continuous feedback?
	How are we helping employees to share what they know about how they do things and how they think about the work? What strategies are we using to evoke thoughts and perceptions that might get ignored?
There is a system for making knowledge readily accessible. The system makes both explicit and tacit knowledge available.	What do our successful people know?
	What do they know that they don't know they know?
	How can we add fresh perspectives to our base?
	Do employees go to the system? Do they seek more than prices and codes? Are they looking for examples of approaches, reports, rationale, commentary? Do they like what they find? Do they contribute?
Employees generously contribute to each other and to the knowledge base.	Do you contribute? Have you hesitated?
	How does the organization combat the tendency to hoard?
	Why do you contribute?
	How does the organization encourage generosity?
	Do employees see themselves as members of communities of practice that transcend unit and even organizational boundaries?
Managers understand that knowledge workers can't be coerced, that they must play a role in determining the meaning of what they do.	Do you solicit the opinions of the people who work for you?
	Do you make information available to people, rather than limit access?
	Do you share decision making?
	Do you make heroes of people who share their intellectual capital?

human resources counseling session to ensuring the existence of an organization that is collecting, maintaining, honoring, and martialing its smarts in service to its customers.

Cognitive Science

Although all practitioners can name the behaviorist B. F. Skinner, it is much harder to get a handle on the cognitivists. As Rita Richey (1986) of Wayne State University points out, cognitivists talk about many things: the readiness of the learner; organization of knowledge, most particularly mental models, or schemata, that people construct to represent what they know; insight; the relationship between computers and intelligence; short-term memory and strategies for ensuring storage and retrieval in long-term memory; individual perspectives on the material or job; and creating meaning by attaching new material to what is already familiar and useful. To all this John Keller (1983) of Florida State adds the issue of motivation, a topic of growing importance because education, training, information, and human resources are increasingly distributed via technology. When there is no commanding instructor or concerned supervisor, what's going on inside the employee influences whether or not he or she will double-click on the Web site or rip open the shrink-wrapped CD-ROM.

What are the implications of cognitive science for you as an analyst? First, you inquire about what is going on inside learners, about their eagerness, readiness, and enthusiasm. Now that employees are no longer considered to be impenetrable "black boxes," front-end inquiry expands to include how individuals perceive the change, opportunity, or problem. Observation won't get at the reasons behind internal processes. Interviews and surveys are critical. Second, you "find" the subject matter, usually during the more expansive training needs assessment. You need to concern yourself with constructing the skeleton or scaffolding for the content and then adding meat to those bones using the perspectives of expert sources. Beyond a focus on what effective people do is the need to unearth what the star performer knows and thinks about. Cognitive science propels us to ask questions about the perspectives of able people as they approach their work. Finally, you must attend to employees' cognitive and metacognitive strategies. This expands the analysis to inquiry about the learning history and proclivities of employees and about their ability to manage their own growth and development. Although a cognitive perspective has been represented throughout this book (see Tables 3.3 and 3.4 and the perspectives of incumbents in Tables 5.1 and 5.2 for a few examples), Table 10.2 offers summary examples.

There are two flavors of cognitivism. The first is objectivist. Famous objectivist cognitivists are Dave Merrill and Ruth Clark. In a nutshell, they believe that you can and should derive and define outcomes. Such outcomes would come from the answers to the questions in Table 10.2. The constructivists, in contrast, doubt the wisdom of articulating outcomes. This position is effectively presented in the *Handbook of Research for Educational Communications and Technology* (Jonassen, 1996).

The constructivist cognitivists raise questions about our ability to set intentions for others. Can it become real and internalized if it is established by one for another? Is knowledge stable? Harkening back to John Dewey, they raise questions about favoring outcomes over process, noting that what matters is the process of seeking, finding, and applying, rather than the acquisition of any body of knowledge.

The constructivists believe that learning takes place through the experiences of the individual learner as she constructs meaning for herself. Whereas an objectivist would present ideas, examples, practices, and feedback, a constructivist would provide access to examples and encourage employees to derive their meaning independently.

Let's look at an example of a pretty typical requirement: "We want managers to become better at dealing with conflict. We think we'd like to offer a class, or something, and maybe some individual coaching sessions. Please get back to me with how we might handle this."

The objectivist's performance analysis might look this: he would attempt to broadly define optimal outcomes associated with handling conflict. What would it look like if managers were in fact better at dealing with conflict? Are there a few acceptable and effective ways we wish to tout? How does an effective manager think about conflict, about getting

TABLE 10.2. TYPICAL QUESTIONS INFLUENCED BY COGNITIVE SCIENCE.

Aspects of Cognitive Science	Analyst Queries
There is concern about feelings. This extends to interest in the readiness, eagerness, and confidence of the workforce.	How do you feel about the _____? Do you share the enthusiasm that management has for it? What do you see as its contributions to the work? Any detriments? Do you understand why it is a priority? Do you feel able to handle it? To pick up the necessary skills? To be good at _____?
There is respect for the thought processes of the workforce.	What do our successful people know and think about? How do successful people think about this?
	When you handle _____ , what comes to mind? How did you decide that?
	How do you think differently about the different kinds of situations you are handling?
	What are the conditions you'll handle using _____?
There is a focus on determining the structure of the subject matter.	Please draw a word picture for me about it.
	Could we sketch it out? What are its parts? What kinds are there?
	What causes it to work? What are the elements of a successful one? What affects what? For that example you just used, why does it work differently than the other three examples?
	We're seeking several opinions on this. Who else would have important things to say about this?
There is an emphasis on the situation or context.	What are the likely challenges? What are the familiar types of challenges? The emerging types? How do they present themselves? How do you recognize one situation from another?
There is concern about the individual's learning proclivities and metacognitive strategies.	How do you like to learn? Are you good at learning on your own? Do you have access to technology for learning and performance support? Have you had positive experiences using technology to learn on your own, answer questions about the organization, provide access to knowledge bases, boost your performance?
	When there's something that changes in your work, are you good at figuring out how to handle the changes?
	Would you describe yourself as good at knowing what you need to know? Good at doing self-assessment? Good at knowing when you've "got" it? Good at knowing what else to do to help you move forward?

positive outcomes from it and reducing the negatives that can result? What kinds of situations come up in which managers need this bag of skills? Where do they tend to mess up?

The objectivist would also seek barriers to successful performance. Why don't managers handle it well now? What gets in their way? What would it take for them to do it more effectively? How do managers feel about this aspect of their work? Answers to these questions would yield a set of outcomes and the drivers associated with them. Then it would be possible to put a solution system in place, including attaching a training needs assessment to those goals that involve skill, knowledge, and motivational concerns.

A constructivist would use analysis differently. Her approach might concentrate on finding numerous examples in the organization and seeking commentary to wrap around those examples. Whereas the objectivist would home in on the common core of attributes associated with a robust and perhaps standard way of approaching conflict, the constructivist is looking for a wide array of options. That array becomes the grist for each individual's experience with handling conflict. This analyst might also use that planning time to establish a rubric that would enable individuals to self-assess their conflict management skills or to observe others in action. The purpose isn't to learn the right way to do it according to the organization or a single expert, but rather to construct a personally useful and realistic approach based on examples and commentary.

Although few organizations have signed up for full-dress constructivist approaches, these perspectives are influential. They lead to more learner control, multiple perspectives, no one right answer, inductive learning and performance processes and experiences, and active involvement by employees in finding answers for themselves for authentic challenges in their world of work.

When I ponder the conflict management example, I see strengths in the objectivist and constructivist approaches. Wouldn't you be inclined to incorporate both in your planning and delivery?

The roadblock for constructivism in most organizations comes from constructivists' reluctance regarding standard organizational approaches, established outcomes or objectives, and evaluation devices based on them. It took years for our profession to sell the importance of being clear about intentions, in performance terms, so that meaningful, targeted practice and measurement can occur. Although the constructivists make many good points, to revisit these issues in a way that might undo our years of effort seems counterproductive.

◆ ◆ ◆

Allison: Well, that's it. Finito. I sure hope the book is helpful. When you work on something for this long, you get to wondering—and worrying.

Allison: Maybe it isn't helpful enough. Maybe I should rewrite Chapter Three, and take another whack at Chapter Six. I've wanted to redo Chapter . . .

Allison: I'll read it one more time. Get one more friend in the business to see what they think.

Allison: Enough already. Like you've said about analysis, and reiterated regarding constructivist approaches, there is no one right answer, no single silver bullet, and of course, no perfect book either. Enough is enough. Wrap it up. Say good-bye.

Allison: OK, OK. 'Bye.

◆ GLOSSARY

Audience analysis

Study that describes the nature of the worker or students. Who are they? What do they already know? Are they confident? Have they volunteered to participate? How many are in the target population? Are they in Chicago or in Togo, Africa? What kinds of technology support are available to them? Are their managers interested in this topic, in their development in this domain?

Barriers

Individual and organizational factors that influence the success of people and organizations; any constraints that are perceived to be getting in the way of performance and accomplishment. For example, the executives lack keyboarding skills, so they avoid e-mail; the lathe operators are not confident that they can handle the shift from analog to digital; the nurses doubt the value of team decision making in the hospital. Barriers are key in defining solutions. Also known as *root causes, causes,* and *drivers.*

Causes

What gets in the way of individual and organizational performance? There are four kinds of causes: absence of skills and knowledge or information, weak motivation, improper environment, and flawed incentives.

It should come as no surprise that the causes of desirable or undesirable performance are unearthed during performance analysis. Causes define solutions. Also known as *drivers, root causes,* and *barriers.*

Cause analysis

Study to determine what gets in the way of individual and organizational performance, and what is involved in developing and maintaining it. See *causes.*

Cognitive task analysis

Detailed study that you do to establish the way able performers think about and approach their work. The study is usually based on interviewing master performers as they do their work. *Cognitive* task analysis concentrates on how the performer contemplates and considers the situation or problem. This activity is resource intensive and most appropriately a part of training needs assessment.

Constructivism

Constructivism is a school of thought that raises questions about the meaning and value of a shared view of optimals. Constructivists question the transmission role played by many in the human resources and training profession, preferring that employees find meaning from active participation with authentic problems and access to many solutions.

Current performance

Information about the contemporary skills, knowledge, perspectives, and activities of individuals in an organization. Specifics about what people now do. Also known as *actuals.*

Drivers

Levers in an organization and person that influence performance. There are many drivers: for example, how much a person knows, how much the person values the work, the person's confidence, the available tools, and an organization's culture, policies, and incentives. The nature of the drivers influences the nature of the solution system that is proposed. See *barriers* and *causes*.

Electronic performance support system (EPSS)

Computer-based system designed to enable the worker to gain access to large amounts of information; it provides opportunities for learning and serves as an expert system that provides advice and coaching through a distinctive and friendly interface. An EPSS integrates information critical to the mission with the coaching and learning resources an employee needs to perform his or her work effectively. An EPSS also applies technology to capture, store, and distribute knowledge throughout an organization. These systems range in application from enriched on-line help systems with wizards and templates to custom-built information systems that employ artificial intelligence to coach and support the user. Also known as interactive performance systems (IPS), performance support systems (PSS), performance support tools (PST), expert systems, and on-line help systems. Some people describe them as souped-up job aids.

Extant data analysis

Analysis of records and files collected by an organization reflecting actual employee performance and its results (for example, sales figures, attendance figures, help desk tapes, callbacks for repair, employee evaluations).

Front-end analysis

Generic term for the study people do to figure out what to do. Synonymous with analysis. Some equate it with performance analysis, which is typically the initial, short-term defining effort driven by a need to understand how to achieve enhanced performance.

Gap

Difference between optimals and actuals, between directions and current performance. Once we have identified a gap, we want to know why it exists or why it is anticipated. A gap analysis for an engineering writing project would target and define the differences between what and how engineers ought to be reporting and writing and what they are in fact doing. That analysis would identify the gap. Also known as the *delta*.

Instructional systems development (ISD)

Systematic approach to training, or the development of instructional systems to meet a specific need. The five stages of ISD are analysis, design, development, implementation, and evaluation. Key factor here is that data from one phase serves as input for the next phase. Analysis, therefore, enlightens subsequent decisions.

Knowledge management

Field of study concerned with the desire to create a culture in which knowledge is paramount. Knowledge moves throughout the organization, hopping boundaries and transcending turf. Thomas Stewart (1997) equated knowledge with wealth in *Intellectual Capital: The New Wealth of Organizations*. More than merely processing objective information, companies committed to knowledge management tap into the tacit and subjective insights of their people and customers and make this wisdom available to strengthen decisions or performances. Innovation is not relegated to the research and development department; the entire organization contributes.

Needs assessment

Systematic study that incorporates data and opinions from varied sources in order to create, install, and evaluate educational and informational products and services. The effort commences as a result of a handoff from the performance analyst and should concentrate on those needs that are related to skill, knowledge, and motivation. Also known as *training needs assessment*.

Objectivism

Contrary to constructivism, objectivists believe that skill, knowledge, expertise, and wisdom are knowable and representable and that one job of the analyst is to gather and represent such knowledge through content analysis, subject matter analysis, or cognitive task analysis, all of which involve determining and expressing optimals so that they can be shared with learners or users.

Optimals

The directions the organization and its people are trying to go, based on what sources wish was happening. Specifics about broad goals and desired skills, knowledge, and perspectives as they relate to a particular task or organizational problem.

Performance analysis

Process by which you partner with clients to identify and respond to problems and opportunities, and to study individuals and the organization to determine an appropriate cross-functional solution system. A systematic and systemic approach to engaging with the client; this is the process by which you determine when and how to use education and information resources.

Performance-centered design

Software materials, typically created from the perspective of the people who use it. Includes a thorough analysis of the end user and his or her work processes as well as continuous user testing, design, and development. This rigorous process with attention to the needs of the "performer" greatly improves the usability, acceptance, and positive impact of the software. It reduces the need to "sell" it within the organization.

Performance drivers

See *drivers, barriers,* and *causes.*

Performance support

Systematic and quantifiable set of processes designed to improve the performance of people and organizations. The practice of providing information and learning resources at the point and time of need to enhance productivity. In contrast to traditional training resources, which may provide education in an environment separate from daily work and for the purpose of enhancing capacity, performance support is intended to provide just-in-time, just-in-place advice and coaching, typically via technology.

Performance technology

Systematic and quantifiable set of processes designed to improve the performance of people and organizations. Focuses on profitable organizational results. The emergence of performance technology is forcing the development of education and training professionals as performance consultants and performance analysts.

Organizational development (OD)

Wide range of interventions, including organizational redesign, group process, culture change, team building, and group feedback systems focusing on ensuring an effective organization. The purview of OD extends to incentives, benefits, and compensation. A growing area of interest to OD professionals is lasting positive change, the goal of any performance system. Performance analysis will often unearth drivers that require the contributions of an OD professional.

Root cause analysis

Study to determine what gets in the way of individual and organizational performance. This term is associated with Peter Senge's important work on the learning organization. See *drivers, causes,* and *barriers.*

Solution system

An array of interventions that, when strategically combined, increase human performance in the workplace. Decisions about the nature of a solution system are based on causes and drivers and determined during performance analysis.

Source

Human or data resource that yields information about actuals, optimals, and causes. Sources include job incumbents, experts, managers, supervisors, and customers. Data resources that yield information about the results of performance can include sales records, accident reports, letters to management, exit interviews, help desk logs, and performance evaluations.

Strategic planning

Systematic study that involves many sources inside and outside the organization or unit to determine *broad* direction or directions. Answers questions about who we are and who we want to be. It also involves admitting who we are *not* and will not be.

Systematic

Characteristic of analysis efforts. Systematic efforts are data driven and are defined, orderly processes by which output from one phase serves as input for the next.

Systemic

Having a focus on relationships within an organization and on how change in one component influences others. Recognizing the individual, team, and organizational aspects of performance and the need for solution systems predicated on causes.

Task analysis

Detailed study you perform to define the actions of master performers. Usually based on observing master performers as they do their work. Often results in a detailed list of activities, elements, and subelements in carefully specified order. Emphasizes the visible actions of able performers. *Cognitive* task analysis enriches task analysis by concentrating on how the performer contemplates and considers the situation or problem. Cognitive task analysis relies on interviews rather than observations. This activity is resource intensive and most appropriately a part of training needs assessment.

Training needs assessment

Systematic study that incorporates data and opinions from varied sources in order to create, install, and evaluate educational and informational products and services. The effort commences as a result of a handoff from the performance analyst and should concentrate on those needs that are related to skill, knowledge, and motivation. Also known as *needs assessment*.

Unattributed information

Characteristic of information provided to customers without your revealing the identity of the source. You do not attach a name to a quote or position. Instead you might say, for example, that the source was an engineer in the Pacific region or a veteran Spanish-speaking social worker or a help desk supervisor from Amsterdam.

◆ RESOURCES FOR PERFORMANCE ANALYSIS

Argyris, C. (1990). *Overcoming organizational defenses.* Needham Heights, MA: Allyn & Bacon.

Argyris, C. (1993). *Knowledge for action: A guide to overcoming barriers to organizational change.* San Francisco: Jossey-Bass.

Bailey-Hughes, B. (1997, May 14). *Implementing survey results* [13 paragraphs]. [On-line]. Available: FTP://ftp.cac.psu.edu/pub/people/cxl18/summary/Implementing

Bandura, A. (1977). Self-efficacy: Toward a unifying theory of behavioral change. *Psychological Review, 84,* 191–215.

Benjamin, S. (1989). A closer look at needs analysis and needs assessment: Whatever happened to the systems approach? *Performance and Instruction, 28*(9), 12–16.

Bolman, L. G., & Deal, T. E. (1991). *Reframing organizations: Artistry, choice, and leadership.* San Francisco: Jossey-Bass.

Bridges, W. (1991). *Managing transitions.* Reading, MA: Addison-Wesley.

Brynjolfsson, E., & Hitt, L. (1996, September 9). The customer counts. *Information Week,* 596, 48–54.

Carlisle, K. (1986). *Job and task analysis.* Englewood Cliffs, NJ: Educational Technology Publications.

Connor, D. R. (1993). *Managing at the speed of change.* New York: Villard Books.

Data mining and statistics: Gain a competitive advantage. (1997). [On-line]. Available: http://www.spss.com/cool/papers/gain.html

Davenport, T. H., & Prusak, L. (1998). *Working knowledge: How organizations manage what they know.* Boston: Harvard Business School Press.

Dean, P. (1996). Editorial: From where come performances in performance technology? *Performance Improvement Quarterly, 9*(2), 1–2.

Dean, P. J., & Ripley, D. E. (Eds.). (1998). *Performance improvement pathfinders: Models for organizational learning systems.* Washington, DC: ISPI.

Dennen, V. P., & Branch, R. C. (1995). *Considerations for designing instructional virtual environments.* (ERIC Document Reproduction Service No. ED 391 489)

Evans, P. B., & Wurster, T. S. (1997, September-October). Strategy and the new economics of information. *Harvard Business Review, 75*(5), 71–82.

Fielding, N. (1994, September). Getting into computer-aided qualitative data analysis data. *ESRC Data Archive Bulletin* [On-line], *57.* Available: http://kennedy.soc.surrey.ac.uk/caqdas/getting.htm.

Fulop, M., Loop-Bartick, K., & Rossett, A. (1997, July). Using the World Wide Web to conduct a needs assessment. *Performance Improvement, 36*(6), 22–27.

Gilbert, T. (1978). *Human competence: Engineering worthy performance.* New York: McGraw-Hill.

Gustafson, K. L., & Branch, R. M. (1997). *Survey of instructional development models* (3rd ed.). Syracuse, NY: ERIC Clearinghouse of Information and Technology.

Hamel, G., & Prahalad, C. K. (1994). *Competing for the future.* Cambridge, MA: Harvard Business School Press.

Hamilton, E. (1993). *The greek way.* New York: Norton.

Hammer, M., & Champy, C. (1993). *Reengineering the corporation.* New York: HarperCollins.

Harless, J. H. (1975). *An ounce of analysis is worth a pound of objectives.* Newnan, GA: Harless Performance Guild.

Harrison, M. I. (1987). *Diagnosing organizations.* Thousand Oaks, CA: Sage.

Hart, I. (1997). ITFORUM PAPER MARCH. In *Instructional Technology Research* [On-line]. Available: http://www.hbg.psu.edu/bsed/intro/docs/qual/index.html

Hatcher, T., & Ward, S. E. (1997). Framing: A method to improve performance analyses. *Performance Improvement Quarterly, 10*(3), 84–103.

Hertzberg, H. (1998, January 5). The narcissus survey. *New Yorker,* 27–29.

Jonassen, D. H. (1991). Objectivism vs. constructivism: Do we need a new philosophical paradigm? *Educational Technology Research and Development, 39,* 5–14.

Jonassen, D. H. (Ed.). (1996). *Handbook of research for educational communications and technology.* Old Tappan, NJ: MacMillan.

Juran, J. M. (1986, May). The quality trilogy. *Quality Progress,* 19–24.

Kelle, U. (Ed.). (1995). *Computer-aided qualitative data analysis.* Thousand Oaks, CA: Sage.

Keller, J. M. (1983). Motivational design of instruction. In C. M. Reigeluth (Ed.), *Instructional design theories and models: An overview of their current status.* Hillsdale, NJ: Erlbaum, 335–382.

Kittleson, M. J. (1995). An assessment of the response rate via the postal service and e-mail. *Journal of Health Values, 18,* 27–29.

Kotler, P., & Andreasen, A. (1987). *Strategic marketing for non-profit organizations* (3rd ed.). Engelwood Cliffs, NJ: Prentice Hall.

Lewis, T., & Bjorkquist, D. C. (1992). Needs assessment—a critical reappraisal. *Performance Improvement Quarterly, 5*(4), 33–53.

Life, love, power, self-image and cars: The official car talk survey results: Introduction. (1997). [On-line]. Available: http://www.cartalk.com/Survey/index.html

Mager, R. M. (1970). *Goal analysis.* Belmont, CA: Pitman Learning.

Mager, R. M. (1984). *Measuring instructional intent.* Belmont, CA: Pitman Learning.

Mager, R. M., & Pipe, P. (1984). *Analyzing performance problems.* Belmont, CA: Pitman Learning.

Mehta, R., & Sivadas, E. (1995). Comparing response rates and response content in mail versus electronic mail surveys. *Journal of the Market Research Society, 37,* 429–439.

Merriam, S. B. (1998). *Qualitative research and case study applications in education.* San Francisco: Jossey-Bass.

Miles, M., & Huberman, A. M. (1984). *Qualitative data analysis.* Thousand Oaks, CA: Sage.

Patton, M. Q. (1987). *How to use qualitative methods in evaluation.* Thousand Oaks, CA: Sage.

PictureTel Corporation. (1996). *Application story: 3M* [On-line]. Available: http://www.pictel.com/apps/applications/3M.html.

Pihlman, M. (1997). Desktop videoconferencing challenge. *New Media* [On-line]. Available: http://www.newmedia.com/NewMedia/95/11/td/vidconf/Desktop_Videoconferencing.html

Rapaport, R. (1996, April-May). The network is the company. *Fast Company, 2,* 116–121.

Richey, R. C. (1986). *The theoretical and conceptual bases of instructional design.* London: Kogan Page.

Robinson, D. G., & Robinson, J. C. (1995). *Performance consulting.* San Francisco: Berrett-Koehler.

Rodgers, E. M. (1983). *Diffusion of innovations* (3rd ed.). New York: Free Press.

Rodriguez, S. R. (1988). Needs assessment and analysis: Tools for change. *Journal of Instructional Development, 11*(1), 23–28.

Rosenberg, M. J. (1990, February). Performance technology working the system. *Training, 27*(2), 42–48.

Rossett, A. (1987). *Training needs assessment.* Englewood Cliffs, NJ: Educational Technology Publications.

Rossett, A. (1990, March). Overcoming obstacles to needs assessment. *Training, 27*(3), 36–41.

Rossett, A. (1996, March). Training and organizational development: Siblings separated at birth. *Training, 33*(4), 53–59.

Rossett, A. (1997, July). That was a great class, but . . . *Training and Development, 51*(7), 18–24.

Rossett, A., & Barnett, J. (1996, December). Designing under the influence: Instructional design for multimedia training. *Training, 33*(12), 33–43.

Rossett, A., & Czech, C. (1996). They really wanna but . . . The aftermath of professional preparation in performance technology. *Performance Improvement Quarterly, 8*(4), 114–132.

Rossett, A., & Downes-Gautier, J. H. (1991). *Handbook of job aids.* San Francisco: Jossey-Bass.

Rummler, G. A. (1986). Organization redesign. In National Society for Performance and Instruction, *Introduction to Performance Technology.* Washington, DC: National Society for Performance and Instruction.

Rummler, G. A., & Brache, A. P. (1990). *Improving performance: How to manage the white space on the organization chart.* San Francisco: Jossey-Bass.

Schein, E. H. (1992). *Organizational culture and leadership* (2nd ed.). San Francisco: Jossey-Bass.

Seels, B., & Glasgow, Z. (1998). *Making instructional design decisions.* Columbus, OH: Merrill.

Senge, P. M. (1990). *The fifth discipline: The art and practice of the learning organization.* New York: Doubleday.

Sleezer, C. M. (1993). Training needs assessment at work: A dynamic process. *Human Resource Development Quarterly, 4*(3), 247–264.

Sherman, R., & Webb, R. (1988). *Qualitative research in education.* London: Falmer.

Stewart, T. A. (1997). *Intellectual capital: The new wealth of organizations.* New York: Doubleday.

Stolovitch, H. D., & Keeps, E. J. (Eds.). (1992). *Handbook of human performance technology: A comprehensive guide for analyzing and solving performance problems in organizations.* San Francisco: Jossey-Bass.

Strauss, A., & Corbin, J. (1990). *Basics of qualitative research.* Thousand Oaks, CA: Sage.

Strauss, A., Schatzman, L., Bucher, R., and Sabshin, M. (1981). *Psychiatric ideologies and institutions.* New Brunswick, NJ: Transaction.

Strayer, J., & Rossett, A. (1994). Coaching sales performance: A case study. *Performance Improvement Quarterly, 7*(4), 39–53.

Swanson, R. A. (1994). *Analysis for improving performance: Tools for diagnosing organizations and documenting workplace expertise.* San Francisco: Berrett-Koehler.

Swenson, R. A., & Rinderer, M. J. (1992). *The training and development strategic plan workbook.* Englewood Cliffs, NJ: Prentice Hall.

Thach, L. (1995). Using electronic mail to conduct survey research. *Educational Technology, 35,* 27–31.

This year's top IT users. (1996, September 9). *Information Week, 596,* 60–69.

Welcome. (1997). [On-line]. Available: http://cac.psu.edu/~cxl18/trdev-l/welcome.html

Wildstrom, S. (1997, June 2). Desktop video: No longer a toy. *Business Week, 22,* n3529.

Witkin, R., & Altschuld, J. W. (1995). *Planning and conducting needs assessments: A practical guide.* Thousand Oaks, CA: Sage.

Zemke, R. (1998, March). How to do a needs assessment when you think you don't have time. *Training, 35*(3), 38–44.

Zemke, R., & Kramlinger, T. (1982). *Figuring things out: A trainer's guide to needs and task analysis.* Reading, MA: Addison-Wesley.

◆ ABOUT THE AUTHOR

Allison Rossett is a professor of educational technology at San Diego State University and a consultant in performance and training systems. She was ISPI vice president for research and development from 1988 to 1990. Rossett has authored two award-winning books, *Training Needs Assessment* and *A Handbook of Job Aids,* and has presented keynote speeches at conferences in this country and around the world. She has also authored articles and conducted studies on the topic of analysis as well as on many others, including new media instructional design, the shift from training to performance, and the fertile and tricky relationship between training and organizational development. Her recent work focuses on global training and performance, Web-based support, and independent learning. A ping-pong champion in her youth, Rossett has recently devoted energy to the challenges of the yo-yo and the ten-minute mile.

◆ INDEX

A

Abacus Concepts, Inc., 125
Actuals: definition of, 34; and determination of optimals, 35; examples of, 33
Agendas, meeting, 113, 114
Amoco, 23; systemic approach to solutions at, 21; virtual performance analyses at, 18–19
Analysis. *See* Performance analysis
Analysis-paralysis, 67–70; and technology, 137
Analysts' experiences: of Coast Guard training program, 191–195; of computers in schools, 186–190; of multinational consulting, 195–199; of on-line training, 205–210; of orientation programs, 199–204
Andersen Consulting, 22, 39; knowledge management at, 216
Annual reports, 80, 95
Assessment instruments, Web site on, 128
AT&T: systemic approach to solutions at, 22; videoconferencing resources from, 125
Audience analysis: definition of, 223; as part of training needs assessment, 23

Authentic communications, 100, 106–107, 108
Automated analysis, 81–82; and discussion group software, 123–124; and electronic surveys, 120–122, 134; and e-mail interviews, 118–119, 134; and focus groups via e-mail, 119–120, 134; and Internet alliances, 127–128; and statistical software, 125–126, 128, 135; and videoconferencing, 124–125

B

Banks, new-product training in, 16–17
Barnett, J., 185, 186; tale from the trenches by, 205–210
Barriers, 19–20
Basics of performance analysis: data, 28, 29–30; directions for the effort, 32–37; drivers, 33–34, 37–47; perspectives of several sources, 28–29; study prior to action, 27, 28; systematic approach, 28, 30, 31; systemic approach, 28, 30–32
Benefits, perceived, 41
Bickham, T., 21; tale from the trenches by, 185, 186, 191–195

Bobenhouse, S., 38
Boeing, generation of feedback at, 77
Brache, A., 142
Bush, S., 47

C

Capacity, definition of, 38
Century 21 International: systemic approach for training at, 31–32; training program goals at, 15–16
Certainty, absolute, 82–83
Chapters in this book, 6,8
Clarification for speedy performance analysis, 70–73, 84
Clark, R., 9, 219
Coast Guards, training program for, 191–195
Cognitive science, 218–222
Communications underpinning analysis, 87–88; authenticity for, 100, 106–107, 108; and executives' perspectives, 100, 105; and experts' perspectives, 100, 102; four principles for, 96; interviews and focus groups, 88–92; and job incumbents' perspectives, 100, 101; observations, 92–95; and perspectives of

Perceived benefits, awareness of, 41

Performance analysis: in context, 12–13; data for, 28, 29–30; definitions of, 10, 13, 26; and directions for the effort, 32–37; and drivers, 33–34, 37–47; for engineers, 68–70; versus needs assessment, 3–5, 49; opportunities for, 51–65; perspectives of several sources for, 28–29; as precursor to needs assessment, 7, 23–25; principles of, 27–32; speed of, 11–12, 67–85; and study prior to action, 27, 28; systematic approach of, 28, 30, 31; systemic approach of, 28, 30–32

Performance Analysis Tool (PAT), 82

Performance appraisals, sample recommendations for, 144

Performance Consulting, 215

Perspectives: and choice of sources, 16–18; executives', 100, 105; experts', 100, 102; on intrusive nature of performance analysis, 107, 109–111; job incumbents', 100, 101; managers', 100, 103; for performance analysis, 28–29; solution partners', 100, 104; of sources, 96–97; technology and access to, 136

Physicians, diagnostics done by, 5, 7

PictureTel, 124, 125

Pipe, P., 9, 44, 215

Planning for effective communications, 96, 111–115

Presentations, slide: on engineering briefings, 160, 165–183; for original customer, 145, 152–160; for upper management, 145, 160, 161–164

Problems, 18; templates for handling, 55, 57, 61–63; as type of opportunity, 53–54

Professional listservs, 123–124, 136; advantages and disadvantages of, 135; Discussion Group for Training and Development (TRDEV-L), 127–128

ProShare, 124, 125

Prusak, L., 215

Public education, technology innovation in, 186–190

Q

Qualis Research Associates, 126

Qualitative data, 129, 131–132

Qualitative software, 126, 135

Quantitative data, 128–129, 130, 131

Quesada, S., 214–215

Questions: from cognitive science perspective, 220; for focused efforts, 34–36; for interviews and focus groups, 90, 91; from knowledge management perspective, 216, 217

Quick-and-dirty analyses, concerns about, 7, 82–84. *See also* Speedy analysis

R

Random sampling, 83

Real estate corporation training programs, 15–16

Real estate development, early opportunity analysis in, 6

Rearview validation, 78

Recommendations, approaches for making, 143–145, 184

Reich, R., 38

Relationship management, 213–215

Relevance of this book, 9

Reporting opportunities, 140–142

Reports, 8; principles for effective, 184; as slide presentations, 145, 152–160, 165–183; to sources, 141–142; for upper management, 160, 161–164; as written briefings, 145, 146–151; as written summaries, 143, 144

Requests handled by human resources: proactive approach toward, 18–19, 78–80; types of, 18

Research Triangle Institute, 126

Researchware Inc., 126

Results, presentation of, 139–140; for executive consumption, 160, 161–164; findings summary example, 143–145; opportunities for, 140–142; oral briefings with slides, 145, 152–160; slide presentation on engineering briefings, 160, 165–183; written report sample, 145, 146–151

Richey, R., 218

Robinson, D. G., 215

Robinson, J. C., 215

Rollout: examples of, 52, 53; operating system, 71, 72–73; templates for handling, 55, 56, 58, 61; as type of opportunity, 52–53

Root cause analysis, 22, 229

Root causes of problems, 32, 210

Rosenberg, M., 9

Rossett, A., 21, 31, 34, 81, 239

Rummler, G., 9, 142, 215

S

Safety programs, development of, 74–76

Sage Publications, Inc., 126

Sampling, random, 83

SAS Institute, 125

SBC, organizational changes at, 4, 23

Schools, technology innovation in: analyst's story about, 186–190; and motivation of teachers, 40

Scott, A., 18

Self-assessment: partnering, 15; solution system, 22

Self-confidence and motivation, 39–41

Senge, P., 43, 81, 215

Sheldon, K., 185, 186; tale from the trenches by, 186–190

Silver bullet approach, 21, 29

Simmons, J., 215

Sivadas, E., 120, 121

Skills: as drivers, 19, 38–39, 44; solutions to lack of, 45

Skinner, B.F., 218

Slide presentations: on engineering briefings, 160, 165–183; for original customer, 145, 152–160; for upper management, 145, 160, 161–164

Smith, K., 18

Solution partners' perspectives, 100, 104